MOSSAD EXODUS

THE DARING UNDERCOVER RESCUE
OF THE LOST JEWISH TRIBE

GAD SHIMRON

gefen
publishing house · בית הוצאה לאור
גפן
JERUSALEM ◆ NEW YORK · Est. 1981

Second edition 2018.
First edition published in 2007 by Gefen Publishing House.

Cover Design: S. Kim Glassman
Typesetting: Marzel A.S. – Jerusalem

ISBN: 978-965-229-403-6

3 5 7 9 8 6 4

Gefen Publishing House Ltd.
6 Hatzvi Street
Jerusalem 9438614, Israel
972-2-538-0247
orders@gefenpublishing.com

Gefen Books
140 Fieldcrest Ave.
Edison NJ, 08837
516-593-1234
orders@gefenpublishing.com

www.gefenpublishing.com
Printed in Israel

Library of Congress Cataloging-in-Publication Data

Names: Shimron, Gad, 1950- author.
Title: Mossad Exodus : the true story of the daring undercover rescue of the
  lost Jewish tribe / Gad Shimron.
Other titles: Havi?u li et Yehude Etyopyah. English
Description: Second edition. | New Jersey : Gefen Publishing House, [2018]
Identifiers: LCCN 2018020672 | ISBN 9789652294036
Subjects: LCSH: Operation Moses, 1984-1985. | Jews--Ethiopia--Migrations. |
  Jewish refugees--Sudan. | Israel. Mosad le-modi?in ?ve-taf?kidim
  meyu?hadim. | Espionage, Israeli--Sudan. | Ethiopia--Emigration and
  immigration. | Israel--Emigration and immigration.
Classification: LCC DS135.E75 S5513 2018 | DDC 362.87089/924063--dc23
LC record available at https://lccn.loc.gov/2018020672

Foreword

For thousands of years, Ethiopian Jews were cut off from the Jewish world. But they kept their identity and religious beliefs in extremely difficult conditions and stuck to an almost messianic dream of reaching Zion.

The story of the immigration of Ethiopian Jews is one of the defining events of the State of Israel.

It began with the trickling in of individuals in the late 1970s. Today, two decades into the twenty-first century, the Ethiopian diaspora no longer exists. The vast majority of this unique community lives in Israel.

An especially exciting aspect of this historic population shift is the Mossad's secret operations to smuggle Ethiopian Jews out of the terrible refugee camps in Sudan and to bring them to Israel in a series of astonishing naval and air operations.

This unusual story of the rescue of refugees from Africa by a Western country willing to endanger planes, ships, the lives of hundreds of soldiers and dozens of secret agents perhaps expresses most of all the uniqueness of the State of Israel and its intelligence service. There is no other example of an intelligence body that is ready to turn the world upside down and to postpone other operations of an intelligence nature only to save refugees.

I was honored to participate in this operation, and in retrospect, I am more proud of the "Brothers Ops" than any of the other operations I took part in.

This book was not written as a history book but as a collection of my own personal memoirs, which I wrote very carefully, fearing that I would downplay the contributions of some of the participants of the operation or magnify those of others.

In describing what happened, I relied solely on the experiences of those turbulent days that were etched in my memory, and naturally, and since many years have passed, I have no doubt that at least some of my colleagues and friends remember those events with different emphases from my own and from different perspectives. At the same time, I am convinced that at least one fact is fully agreed upon by all: the period in which we participated in the complex and exciting operation of the rescue of Ethiopian Jews from Sudan was the most exciting in our lives.

I dedicate the book to the thousands of anonymous heroes of the Beta Yisrael who suffered unbearable hardships and fulfilled their dream of coming to Zion, as well as to all those Israelis who enthusiastically enlisted in the long and dangerous campaign of bringing Ethiopian Jews to Israel.

Gad Shimron
2018

Chapter 1

The Sudanese television newscaster, who somehow always managed to appear emaciated and exhausted, started reading the final newscast summarizing the events of Sunday, January 6, 1985, in a monotonous voice. A generator clattering in the small courtyard outside made it possible for us to follow the news despite frequent power failures. "It's the fifth one today," someone commented angrily. As is customary in Arab countries, the first five minutes were devoted to giving an account of the daily activities of the ruler, General Jaafar Nimeiri. Nimeiri here, Nimeiri there, and not one word about the palpable tension in the streets of Khartoum, the persistent rumors of an impending military coup, and not even a squeak about the hottest story in the international press that week.

"Operation Moses is over," I heard the Israeli government announcement through an earphone plugged to a portable radio, which for reasons known only to signal corps experts, was able to pick up, of all things, Kol Israel's news programs in Khartoum every evening. The newscaster's deep voice gave him away as Zvi Salton, a colleague from my days in Kol Israel, Israel's official radio network. He read out the official Israeli government statement, with a quote from Shimon Peres, the prime minister, about Operation Moses, the remarkable rescue of thousands of Ethiopian Jews who were stranded in Sudan.

That night in Khartoum, we didn't know that the citizens of Israel had already seen footage of dark-skinned Jews alighting from jetliners, bewildered by the host of television cameras and glaring spotlights, still not grasping that they had reached their coveted destination.

We, a small group of Mossad agents staying in Khartoum and

5

dealing with the more covert aspect of the rescue operation, were aware of other images: small, overloaded rubber dinghies making their way to an Israel Navy vessel waiting beyond the coral reefs and the horizon, and air force C-130 Hercules transports landing in the middle of the night at an improvised landing strip in the desert, loading up hundreds of famished refugees.

But now, through the earphone, I could only pick up the last chords of Operation Moses, including, as expected, some reaction by politicians, and sharp criticism from those who decried the lifting of the veil of secrecy from the operation, causing it to be suspended the previous day.

"Once again, lousy politicians and nosy journalists," someone quipped. "You mean 'again,' not just 'once again,'" I corrected him with a broad smile, knowing that the friendly taunt was intended mostly for myself.

"It's rather strange to be in Khartoum and hear from Israel about the suspension of an operation which only we know is still going on," said the know-it-all technician, who managed to keep our equipment functioning even in the impossible conditions prevailing in Sudan. "You're a journalist yourself," he added, grinning from ear to ear. "The day after tomorrow you'll sit poker-faced in front of your computer screen at *Maariv* newspaper, while everyone around you keeps talking about this astounding operation and the courage of the indefatigable Mossad men. Tell me you're not suffering from a split personality," he challenged, still smiling, and even before I had a chance to respond, he launched into a series of complaints about having been ordered to stay behind with our small group to await further instructions.

The following day, at the filthy and derelict Khartoum Airport, on my way back to Europe, after countless luggage checks and poking by jittery police and soldiers, another scene came back to me, from another airport three years earlier...

Then, in the spring of 1982, we were standing at the southern wall of the arrival hall at Israel's Ben-Gurion Airport, looking like a bunch of tourists returning from a successful holiday abroad.

We were five men, aged thirty to forty, well bronzed, smiling and laughing. Sharp-eyed bystanders could perhaps have discerned a minor difference between us and other Israelis in the same age group: the complete lack of a paunch, one of Mr. Israel's main trademarks.

Approaching us from a side room was a man, aged about fifty, wearing thick-lensed glasses, under a shock of white hair that was intended to conceal a widening bald spot. He was then the commander of our unit in the Mossad, which handled the extricating of Jews from countries where they were threatened. His name was Ephraim.

Ephraim shook our hands with warmth, and to our surprise gave each and every one of us a slap on the back, a gesture totally out of character for this taciturn man. "I have come from the office of Menachem Begin," he said. "He heard with great interest the report about your covert activities in Sudan and was deeply impressed with your dedication in the face of all the problems and hitches. The prime minister questioned me closely and asked me to relay his greetings to you." Taking a folded piece of paper from his pocket he began reading: "To our valiant boys, who operate in the desolate desert, risking their lives, under difficult conditions, to bring the Ethiopian Jews to Zion...."

I am no longer certain this was the exact text, but that was the spirit. The remainder of the missive has long been erased from my gray cells, but I will never forget the roaring laughter his words elicited from us and the expression of shock on his face. Ephraim was one of the Mossad "old school" officials. I don't know whether he expected us to jump to attention the moment we realized he was carrying a message from the prime minister, who technically was our direct boss, or merely expected us to sit back and listen politely, but it was plain the last thing he expected was our rambunctious laughter.

We couldn't tell him that we couldn't care less about Begin, and that his flowery prose should really be relegated to the Mossad's history section. After three months of hard work, replete with adventures and dangers in Sudan, in total isolation from our families and what was happening back home — this was the time of the Israeli pullback from the Sinai Peninsula and growing tension along the Lebanese border — all we wanted to do was to get through passport control quickly and return home.

"Bye, Hafisniks, and see you in the next operation," I told my colleagues, taking leave of Danny, commander of the operation, whose work on behalf of the State and Ethiopian Jews left him no time to deal with his marital problems; Ruby, the former Navy SEAL, who even at a distance of thousands of miles never stopped keeping tabs on the fluctuating stock market where he had invested the money he received in compensation for the home he had to leave in Sinai; Shlomo Pomeranz, a doctor, who loved downing Coca Cola in commercial quantities and greasing up in machine oil; Marcel, who had seen a lot of action and always ate with his mouth open; and Shmulik the diver, a knife buff from Eilat who always managed to get out of tough situations.

"Hafisniks?" Ephraim queried.

"It's an acronym for Haka's Forces in Sudan," I replied, hastening to leave the terminal while humming what I could remember of a popular song of that name. Haka was the nickname of General Yitzhak Hofi, then head of the Mossad.

As we parted with "*Lehitraot* (see you again)," we weren't really convinced that it would happen any time soon. In the spring of 1982 we didn't believe that the State of Israel would continue the effort to rescue Ethiopian Jews stranded in Sudan. There were far more serious problems to tackle at the time: completion of the withdrawal from Sinai, runaway inflation and threats of war along the northern border, which drew warnings from Begin and Raful (Lieutenant General Rafael Eitan, the army chief of staff) to Hafez Assad, the Syrian president.

Chapter 2

I reached Sudan for the first time at the end of 1981. The hot air rushed into the plane as soon as the doors opened, making it clear beyond doubt that we were in Africa. "Today it's relatively cool, only 35 degrees (95 Fahrenheit)," announced the captain of the KLM airliner that brought us from Amsterdam.

"Welcome to Sudan," declared a huge sign across the facade of the Khartoum Airport terminal, which looked like a replica of the old terminal at Israel's Lydda Airport, an elongated structure with a small control tower in the center. "Hats off to the British Empire," I told Ruby, who came with me on that flight. "The architect in charge of planning saved a lot of money for the UK treasury, and recycled the Lydda Airport plans."

Ruby muttered something in "Pinglish," Palestinian English. He was a little drunk. So was I. This was because of the pressure headquarters had put on us to get to Sudan as quickly as we could and present ourselves at a holiday village leased for us from the local tourist office by our cover company, called Navco. Such was the pressure from headquarters that we boarded the first flight for Khartoum that day, which was fully booked except for two first-class seats. "The chief accountant will explode, but there's no choice. Headquarters wants quick action, so they may just as well pay up," we comforted each other.

"We slightly overdid the drinking. That last gin and tonic was absolutely over the top," said Ruby, burping, prompting a stewardess to smile. During the eight-hour flight she and other members of the cabin crew plied us with drinks as soon as they noticed that our glasses had dried up. Naturally, we never refused.

"Bye-bye, Europe," I said quietly as I left the clean cabin to go down the dirty, beat-up stepladder leading onto the hot asphalt and the walk toward Sudan's international airport arrivals terminal.

The friendly Sudanese who waited for us at the arrivals hall, which was a Third-World *balagan* (a chaotic mess), was the one, as we had told the check-in clerk in Schiphol Airport, who had arranged for our entry visas to Sudan. The clerk had refused to sell us tickets because we had no visas stamped in our passports. She relented only after we signed a lengthy declaration in Dutch and English to the effect that we were responsible for any expense, including the return flight tickets, should the Sudanese turn us away.

"Welcome to Sudan and I hope you bring good business with you," said Hassan, the tall and energetic employee of the Sudanese Tourist Corporation, who welcomed us. He had been named only a few weeks earlier as representative of our straw company in Khartoum, and believed that we were the harbingers of a new era in tourism for his country and a dramatic change in his own personal financial situation.

Hassan took our passports, warmly shook the hand of the immigration officer, and disappeared with him into a side room. Two days of contacts with the local bureaucracy went by before I learned that the warm handshake between Hassan and the officer was a splendid example of the customary greeting style between a client and a supplier of a service, and that during this gesture a banknote makes its way into the hand of the supplier, the amount of which depends on the type of service sought and the rank of the supplier.

By the time Hassan returned with our passports, which naturally did not bear the Menorah emblem nor were they issued by the government printer in Jerusalem (Sudan was then, as it is today, an enemy country), I managed to survey the scene around me. The luggage of the KLM passengers arrived behind an old tractor pulling a number of rickety carts. A battalion of porters took the suitcases into the arrivals hall and laid them on a conveyor belt — motionless, of course, due to an operator's error or lack of a vital spare part. The term "maintenance" is not common to most Third World languages, and one could safely assume that this conveyor belt had broken down only weeks after being inaugurated in an impressive ceremony.

The passengers on our flight were divided into two groups: whites and local blacks. The whites in turn were divided into two subgroups: holders of hard currency and bearers of Communist block passports. The whites had no business at all with the local clerks. Each of them was awaited by a fixer standing in the hall, whether on behalf of his embassy (socialist passengers) or someone like our Hassan, who took care of all the local arrangements. In any case, the more respectable-looking or wealthy locals also resorted to fixers. The rest, a small group of Sudanese bereft of funds or contacts, had to go through hell — frightfully slow passport control, a health check and a nosy customs officer who had to be bribed — before being reunited with their families who waited outside the hall.

A huge dilapidated fan, dating to the days of British rule, rotated slowly and ineffectually under the ceiling. It had probably looked down on the bald pate of Menachem Begin, who made a stopover in Khartoum in the 1950s on his way from Israel to South Africa to speak to his Beitar movement sympathizers in Johannesburg. Until 1956, Sudan was under British control, and holders of Israeli passports were able to get off the aircraft during stopovers.

And it was the same Menachem Begin who in December 1981 caused Ruby and myself to stand in the same derelict hall at Khartoum Airport — under a gleaming picture of President Jaafar Nimeiri in a general's uniform adorned with medals for unknown victories — waiting for one of the Sudanese ruler's functionaries to condescend to stamp an entry visa in our passports, with Hassan's able intervention of course. All of this was accomplished in return for a sum that did not dent Israel's defense budget, but was certainly impressive by local standards.

Chapter 3

One of Menachem Begin's first moves after his surprising victory in the 1977 general elections was to summon the head of the Mossad, Yitzhak (Haka) Hofi.

After listening attentively to Haka's defense review, he turned to him with an unusual request: "We know that thousands of Falasha, Ethiopian Jews, are desperate to immigrate to Israel. They are starving, persecuted by the authorities and tormented by their neighbors. I ask you to use the Mossad to find a way to bring these dear Jews to Israel. Bring the Ethiopian Jewry to me."

The historical truth is that for many years Israel had not regarded the Ethiopian Jews as Jews. Very few of them had immigrated to Israel over the years. The orthodox establishment regarded them only as an exotic tribe which might be linked to Judaism one way or another. This was despite the wealth of information that proved them categorically to be part of the Jewish people. They spurn the name Falasha, a derogatory term meaning "people without land," and call themselves "Beta Yisrael."

In 1910, the researcher Jacques Faitlovitch published a book, *A Journey through Abyssinia*, in which he describes in great detail his meetings with Jews in the farthest villages of the distant kingdom. He heard from them about the past glory of Ethiopian Jews, when they controlled a large kingdom. Because their isolation from other Jewish communities lasted for centuries, he said, they jealously kept the Sabbath, laws of cleanliness (*tahara*), dietary laws (*kashrut*) and circumcision (*mila*), but the customs of putting on phylacteries (laying *tefillin*), wearing skullcaps or any other headgear and use of prayer shawls (*tallit*) were alien to them. So, too, were the Hanukah and Purim holidays.

The Ethiopian Jews go by the laws of the Torah (the Five Books of Moses) alone, and are not familiar with the later Talmud and the body of oral studies. Their holy books are written in an ancient local dialect, Ge'ez, which only the religious leaders of the community, the *kessim*, are able to read.

Faitlovitch had no doubt that they were Jews. Other researchers who dug into the ancestry of Ethiopian Jews have come up with differing theories as to their origins. One claimed they descend from the Jewish community that lived in Egypt in the days of the First Temple. Another traced them to Yemen. At the beginning of the twentieth century the Ethiopian Jews were estimated to be a hundred thousand strong, but their numbers dwindled with some converting to Christianity because of religious persecution and economic pressure. The converted Jews were called Falashmura, and many of them have maintained family contacts with their Jewish brethren, who barely numbered twenty-five thousand by the late 1970s.

Despite the opposition of the religious establishment, several dozen Ethiopian Jews managed to immigrate to Israel after its establishment in 1948. This included some who had been trained in Israel as teachers or youth group leaders. These returned to their villages in Ethiopia at the behest of their leaders and heads of the Jewish Agency.

In the early 1960s, during Haile Selassie's imperial reign, when relations between Ethiopia and Israel were close, Israeli representatives took up the issue of immigration of Ethiopian Jews to Israel with the aging emperor, but much to their surprise they were turned down. Selassie was thoroughly familiar with the Zionist movement. After his country fell to fascist Italy, he spent two years in exile in Jerusalem. "In Ethiopia there are seventy different peoples, Christian, Muslim and Jewish. They are all Ethiopians. If I let the Falasha leave for Israel, how can I turn down requests from Somali tribes to reunite with their brethren? And what shall I tell the Eritreans? I am everyone's father, and I want this huge family to remain united," the emperor, also known as the Lion of Judah, told the emissaries from Jerusalem.

The emperor, who resided in a sumptuous palace in Addis
Ababa, totally isolated from his people, perceived himself as the
father of the Ethiopian nation. But in 1974 he was toppled by conspirators headed by Mengistu Haile Mariam, a young and ruthless
army officer. The emperor himself died — allegedly of illness — in
1975.

The emperor's removal and the seizing of power by the military
brought about a change in status between Jerusalem and Addis
Ababa, pushing the two countries' relations out of the limelight
and away from newspaper headlines. At the behest of the new,
Communist-leaning regime, the relationship was mainly based
on military assistance and Israeli officers acting as advisors to the
Ethiopian army, which was battling insurgents in the Eritrea and
Tigre provinces seeking to break away from Ethiopia and gain their
independence.

Mengistu, a dictator who did not regard himself as the "father
of the nation" — his soldiers were carrying out atrocities against
their "brethren" from Eritrea — agreed to allow Jews to emigrate
to Israel in exchange for military equipment, but only on condition that the deal was kept secret. Towards the end of 1977, Israeli
Air Force Boeing 707 aircraft flew military equipment into Addis
Ababa and flew Ethiopian Jews back to Israel. This was to be a
large-scale operation with many flights. However, the operation
was terminated after two flights only, because of the urge of one of
our senior politicians to blabber away, a precursor to the official
prattle that cut off Operation Moses seven years later. Those two
flights carried 125 Ethiopian Jews to Israel.

That politician was Israel's then foreign minister Moshe Dayan,
who said during an interview in Switzerland that Israel was sup-
plying weapons to the Mengistu regime and helping him preserve
the unity of the country. No one knows what prompted Dayan to
open his mouth in Zurich, of all places, or why he spoke about the
Ethiopian issue.

The great tragedy of Ethiopian Jewry was that just when the
immigration and communication channels were cut off, the chief

Sephardic rabbi had found enough Halachic evidence to determine that they were indeed Jews. At the same time, he hedged his decision in several key areas that had prevented the religious establishment from recognizing them as Jews in the full sense of the word. This decision was responsible ten years later for the many obstacles that hindered the full integration of Ethiopian Jews into Israeli society, as the religious establishment demanded that immigrants undergo a series of humiliating ceremonies before they could become part of the Israeli populace.

The bottom line of the chief rabbi's decision was, however, that they were Jews covered by the Law of Return, which granted automatic Israeli citizenship to newly arrived Jewish immigrants. Menachem Begin, who reached the premiership after years in the political opposition wilderness, not least because of the support of Sephardic Jews, saw himself committed to relocating the members of that remote community to Israel, whatever the cost may be.

Chapter 4

Menachem Begin's wish to see Ethiopian Jews in Israel was handed down to Danny as a complex operational order, very low on operational intelligence — that is, it was low on the priority list and there was very little data already collected on the region.

"Because of the civil war in Ethiopia, we have no way of reaching the Jewish concentrations there," it was explained to Danny. "According to reports from UN relief agencies operating in Sudan, there is a flow of refugees out of the battle zones to makeshift camps in Sudan. We've got to take advantage of the situation to find out if there are any Jews among the refugees. We have received a message from one Ethiopian Jew, calling himself Ferede, asking for help to get out of Sudan. Go to Sudan, look for him, and together, the two of you try to locate Jews. At the same time, you may succeed in reaching Tigre and Gondar Provinces in Ethiopia, where Jews live."

A closer study of the explanation Danny received makes one fact plain: from the point of view of the Mossad, Sudan, the largest country in Africa, was nothing but a black hole. But Danny is not your average Israeli. Thanks to him and others like him, the Mossad has been able to do the impossible at times, including operating in black holes.

Danny was born in South America to French parents, immigrated to Israel as a teenager, and in no time became more Sabra (native-born Israeli) than a Sabra. He served in the paratroops, successfully graduated officer training, and because of his many qualifications and his full command of French, was recruited to the Mossad shortly after his military service.

He embarked on a promising career that might have taken him to the top in the Mossad, but his career was truncated because of his involvement in drafting a brief letter that created a storm in the corridors of the prestigious espionage organization.

In the early 1970s, ten Mossad employees, mostly young and concerned, drafted a document decrying corruption and cronyism among some of the more senior members of the organization. "The Letter of the Ten" was eventually leaked to the press and became source material for dozens of "exposés" about the Mossad.

Mossad employees, like other employees of the defense establishment, including army officers and Shabak (domestic security) agents, are forbidden by law to unionize. The head of the Mossad is not only the boss, but also looks after his employees' work conditions like a father. His door is supposed to be open to any employee seeking to air grievances, but phenomena like the Letter of the Ten were considered sacrilege, akin to an unlawful gathering.

This drew a prompt and decisive response from the top brass. No sooner did the men sign the document, than they were classified as "troublemakers" or "renegades."

One of the signatories, who reached the Mossad after lengthy military service, quit and rejoined the army. Another member reached his own conclusions, switched to the academic world and has since been doing well at Tel Aviv University, trying in his own way to craft solutions to the Israeli-Palestinian conflict. Yet another signatory, Yariv, whose enemies spared no effort to blacken his name, resigned and at a relatively advanced age successfully completed the Israeli Air Force flight training course. Ironically, ten years after his departure from the Mossad he joined the ranks again to be in charge of the second phase of the operation to rescue Ethiopian Jews from Sudan. The remainder of the signatories, who decided to stay on despite being marked, at least in the eyes of the directors, had to make do with minor and secondary tasks until the storm passed.

To my mind, the Ethiopian Jews living in Israel today owe their repatriation to the Letter of the Ten. Danny, whose promotion had been frozen, was called upon to be in charge of what appeared to the Mossad brass to be a minor, marginal, almost hopeless operation, which was relegated to the lackluster unit dealing with extrication of Jews from countries where they are in distress.

It was common knowledge in the Mossad that this unit attracted troublemakers, idlers and soon-to-be-retired employees seeking a cushy and non-binding posting abroad, thereby earning a last promotion to increase their pension benefits.

Had command of the operation been given to someone else, it's highly doubtful that even one Ethiopian Jew would have left Sudan and reached Israel. But Danny epitomized operational initiative, cunning, proper reading of the situation, and ardent belief in the importance of the mission, stemming from values alien to most Mossad employees. He was one of the few observant men among Mossad operatives, and the small skullcap atop his blond curls was highly noticeable in Mossad hallways. He would consult with rabbis when he faced major decisions. "I received dispensation from Chief Ashkenazic Rabbi Shlomo Goren to eat nonkosher food and drive on the Sabbath in Sudan, because we are dealing there with a matter of life and death," he said once while wolfing down seafood (forbidden by Jewish dietary laws) which even to novices did not appear to be anything close to kosher.

His outstanding personality traits concealed other, less positive aspects, from the Mossad's point of view: misplaced frivolity, glossing over technical details and sudden shifts between admirable flexibility and almost unbearable obstinacy.

But Danny was the unstoppable force that would persist until he moved the unmovable object, and this indeed happened, time and again.

Chapter 5

"I've been through a lot," Danny told me one evening as we were lying under a Toyota pickup truck somewhere in a remote and unchartered part of Sudan, in a desperate effort to catch some shade before our designated radio rendezvous with headquarters. "But no scriptwriter, however deranged, could come up with a plot close to what I went through during the initial phases of this operation."

Danny went to Khartoum in the guise of a research anthropologist. "I thought that this would make it possible for me to reach places usually unfrequented by whites," he said.

Sudan is the largest country in Africa, occupying over two and a half million square kilometers, approximately a hundred times the size of Israel. It is a country rich in landscapes and natural resources that brings up the rear on the list of the world's poorest countries because of a corrupt leadership, epitomizing Murphy's law: "If anything can go wrong, it will." The scorching desert wind coupled with the local mentality, and the fact that Sudan lacked strategic importance — substantial quantities of oil would only be discovered much later on — and thus received only a pittance in foreign aid, all combined to obliterate in a few years' time the vestiges of the culture of governance and public order the British had tried to impart during their rule.

"In Khartoum of the late 1970s and early 1980s the joy of independence had long been forgotten, giving way to a festering decline into a deep economic crisis," Danny said. "From time to time, there were reports about an oil strike in the south or an idea to use the fertile Nile land to turn Sudan into a giant granary for the entire Arab world. But on the ground, except for solemn cornerstone-laying ceremonies, nothing much happened in Khartoum. Several days went by before I adjusted to the slow-moving Sudanese reality, which matches the flow of the Nile. Even a minor matter, like renting a dependable car with a good supply of gasoline and oil, was a complicated and expensive logistic effort. I made contacts in the diplomatic community, with members of United Nations aid agencies as well as various Ethiopian exiles. All in all, despite the economic crisis, for anyone with dollars Khartoum was a place where living was not bad at all, including diplomatic cocktails, fancy meals and other festivities.

"One day," continued Danny, "I was invited to dinner at the residence of a Western ambassador. And who should they seat me by? An anthropologist! He had researched tribes in Papua New Guinea, taught university, danced with Indians in the thick of the jungles of the Amazon and toured around the world — quite unlike me, who had only read a fake-your-way-through-anthropology guide. Naturally he showed an interest in me, asked who I was and what research I was doing. I knew that if I got drawn into a professional discussion, I would blow my cover. 'With your permission,' I told him while raising a glass of superb French wine, 'let's not talk shop for one evening.' He seemed to like the idea."

In the south of Sudan, battles and skirmishes with the local underground were going on, and the north was undergoing an economic crisis, but compared with the situation in the neighboring countries — Uganda, Ethiopia and Chad — Sudan in the late 1970s and early 1980s provided another proof of the validity of Einstein's theory of relativity: the region was an island of stability and quiet in East Africa. Millions of destitute people crossed international boundaries, which appeared only on maps, to live in makeshift camps, straw huts, humble tents and tin shacks, awaiting help.

In Khartoum, Danny was able to develop contacts with representatives of various aid agencies who tried to channel funds for the millions of refugees and offer them aid through the corrupt Sudanese officialdom. He located Ferede, who told him that all he wanted was to reach Israel as fast as possible. "I had a heart-to-heart chat with him and succeeded in convincing him that he had to help us pull his brethren out of Sudan." Ferede agreed, without knowing that another eighteen months would go by before his dream would come true.

Danny and Ferede scoured the refugee camps around Khartoum and the refugee concentrations along the Ethiopian border. In the Gedaref and Kassala villages there were at least one million refugees in makeshift camps. Hygiene was terrible, and the fact that no epidemics broke out was a tribute to massive assistance from the West, which, as is customary in Third World countries, also made its way in part to the black market.

Nimeiri's secret police agents were all over the place, keeping tabs on the refugees, whose infighting did not cease even in exile. Various factions of Eritreans and Tigreans in the camps continued to kill each other. A representative of one of the underground movements also tried to arrest Danny. They suspected him of being an agent of Mengistu, the hated Ethiopian ruler.

And through all this mess, Danny and Ferede went around by themselves, without any help, and in circumstances that would have caused any average Mossad man to throw up his hands in the air and report back to headquarters: "Sorry, have found no Jews."

But Danny did not give in. When he was detained for questioning by suspicious policemen, he escaped from the interview room, later shifting the focus of his activities to another area until things calmed down.

Sudanese secret police never stopped sniffing around him and among the refugees in an attempt to control what was going on in the camps. The Jews did not identify themselves as Jews for fear of the Sudanese police and reprisals by local citizens. "In the camps, it was near impossible to tell apart Christians, Muslims and Jews," recalled Ferede years later. After countless adventures, Ferede managed to locate two Jews, but they were loath to be unnecessarily exposed. It took a great deal of effort to convince them that he was a Jew who had come to rescue them. They finally agreed to help him and others.

The first contact had been made.

But most of the Ethiopian Jews, many of whom had never seen a white person before, categorically refused to believe that Danny was Jewish. "I am Falasha, a white Falasha," he told them. But his words still failed to breach the wall of suspicion. "Only after I attended one of their prayer sessions did they believe that I was a Jew, a peculiar one, but a Jew nonetheless."

From that moment, the rescue of the Ethiopian Jews from Sudan became Danny's life mission. His enthusiasm was contagious. He did not hesitate to recruit potential candidates to help.

Chapter 6

In the fall of 1981 I was in the process of being fired from the Mossad for the second time in my life. I was only thirty-one years old.

I got divorced a year earlier. I was among thousands of other Israelis who rushed to get married after the 1973 Yom Kippur War, and found themselves gracing the divorce statistics six or seven years on. It was a painful and complicated divorce, but despite the personal crisis I somehow managed to keep my head above water while waiting for an important course, which was vital to anyone aspiring to a career in the Mossad. But soon I found out that my name had been dropped from the candidate list because I was a divorced man.

"Move to a desk job, get involved in administration until you get married again," I was told by Human Resources in response to the shocked look on my face. They came up with an inane explanation: "Please understand, we have had cases of divorced and single people assigned to sensitive jobs abroad, who got involved with local women."

I controlled my anger with difficulty. "I know many married people in the Mossad who got involved with women on the outside, including some of the more senior brass I happen to work with," I said. "You know as well as I do that not a few Mossad operatives abroad only go home for a shower and a change of shirt." This was an exact description of the marital status of one of those who tried to explain to me why my divorce impeded my advancement. "And besides, I'm familiar with the Mossad assignment roster and nowhere does it say that you have a mandate to deal with marital issues."

This furious retort reverberated in the hallways and only reinforced my reputation in the Mossad as a troublemaker, one who refuses to toe the line and asks a lot of pointed questions. The "remarks" section in my personal file was one of the most extensive in all of the Mossad.

I was recruited to this secret organization for the first time in the mid-1970s. It was unplanned, the result of a friend's recommendation. In those days the name "Mossad" was spoken only in a whisper. Everything then was steeped in secrecy. To my surprise, within a few months, I found myself serving in the Mossad's spearhead operational unit.

But on recruitment day I still had no idea where I was heading. I didn't know that along with me, a handful of carefully chosen people had also been drafted, after the previous operational unit was disbanded because of poor human relations.

Apparently, they thought well of my qualifications. How else can you explain why I was accepted, even though I was already a working journalist? In Mossad terminology, "journalist" is synonymous with "a dangerous element that must be avoided at all costs."

At the time of my recruitment, I was majoring in History and Far Eastern Studies at Jerusalem's Hebrew University, and working for a living as a cub reporter on Israel Radio's "*Hayom Hazeh* (this day)" daily news show. I joined the radio, just as I later joined the Mossad, quite by accident. It was all because of a party I hosted in 1972 with my flatmate Shmuel Tal. Half the student body was there. Late that night, I was groggy with vodka and went out on the balcony to take in some fresh mountain air. Two men were standing in a corner arguing about some military maneuver during World War II. As the topic was familiar to me, and being slightly drunk, I didn't wait to be invited and joined the conversation with a key sentence: "What are you talking about? In Africa, under Rommel, the Germans kept barely four divisions, whereas on the Russian front they had nearly two hundred." The men were astounded by the stranger who was barging in on their conversation, and also by my knowledge, and within minutes we became engrossed in a drunken talk about armored tactics in World War II.

"Who are you?" asked one of them.

"Very pleased to meet you," I responded. "I'm your host."

"Perhaps you want to work for Israel Radio? We need knowledgeable young men fluent in foreign languages. By the way, I'm Rafi Unger."

Rafi Unger was at the time one of the pillars of the radio's News and Current Affairs department. That's how I joined the radio. Rafi was killed a year later during the 1973 Yom Kippur War.

As for my joining the Mossad, that joyful moment was preceded by a lengthy and tiresome screening process that included endless tests and examinations. Despite my reverence for the organization that let me join its ranks, I also brought a considerable amount of cynicism and skepticism with me, which may have been the product of my short stint as a newsman and kept me from becoming a blind admirer of the organization.

Next came a difficult and arduous training course, both fascinating and stimulating, at the end of which I found myself part of a tiny group of marvelous men and women. Together, we did amazing things, which for the sake of Israel's security must still remain under wraps. It was an interesting period that lasted for over two years, ending when the Broadcast Authority started inquiring about its employee from the news department, who had been lent for temporary duty to the Mossad. I was ready to continue serving with the Mossad. However, my pay scale with the radio was too high for the taste of the Mossad manpower honchos. They offered me a full-time job on a much lower scale.

I declined, and the Mossad refused to compromise. And so, at the end of 1977, I found myself back in Jerusalem, saddled with a wife, a baby and work on the radio which bored me to tears. I landed in the office during the heady days of Egyptian president Anwar Sadat's visit to Israel and the beginning of the first peace talks with an Arab nation, and soon realized that I was in deep trouble. Hardly a day went by without an "exciting" story being aired that I knew more about than the most senior correspondents. And while everyone kept wondering how Sadat ended up suddenly on the Knesset podium, I was forced to hold my tongue and keep to myself everything I knew about Moshe Dayan's secret forays to Morocco, which had paved the way for this historical visit.

Fourteen months into my work for the Broadcast Authority, I found myself yet again inside the "Mossad family" — the term of endearment used by members of the agency — and again thanks to a random meeting with a senior official, this time in the streets of a European city. He was then in charge of manpower at the Mossad. I was in Europe on a wild trip with my wife and the baby to clear our heads and decide what to do next.

"After hunting elephants it's pretty boring smashing cockroaches with the tip of your shoe," I told him after he inquired about my health. Then, out of the blue he asked if I wanted to come back to the Mossad. After brief negotiations that saw me make a small concession — one pay scale less than I had with the radio and on his part a promise for the future ("You will be posted to the unit you want and take the first Arabic course to open") — I returned to the "family" fold. I completed the intensive Arabic course successfully, perhaps due to the special atmosphere that suffused the course or to the antiquated but effective teaching style still practiced in the *heder* (an ultraorthodox religious school for small boys found today in religious Israeli neighborhoods like Bnai Brak or Mea Shearim), requiring you to learn everything by heart.

Afterwards I was assigned to another job, which included short and very interesting missions to new places, tiding me over until a more advanced course began. But then I was informed that my candidacy was being dropped because of my divorce. Almost concurrently, at the end of the summer of 1981, I ran into Danny, the blond, religious operative, in the Mossad building.

"Gadash," he called me by one of my nicknames. "What are you doing? Listen, I'm going to mount a mammoth operation in Sudan. I need someone like you, who has field experience, languages and loves the ocean. It fits you like a glove. Are you coming?"

I tempered his enthusiasm. I told him that I was on my way out, had a letter of resignation in my pocket, and that I wasn't willing to work in the Israeli spy agency, whose top brass believe that sitting at a desk is a proper solution to personal problems and a handsome boost to a career.

"Drop the nonsense, you and your resignations," he said, slapping me on the shoulder. "This job is made for you. I'm going directly to the boss to have you reinstated."

To this day, I don't know whether Danny took up the matter with Mossad head Yitzhak Hofi, or got stuck at a lower level. However hard he tried he couldn't get my superiors to change their minds. I must have made too much trouble, using the word "no" too often. Some recalled the limericks I composed about my direct boss, a certified idiot to my mind, but not in the eyes of the system. My claims were vindicated several years later, when the idiot almost brought about a giant operational fiasco, which was averted only through massive help from friends.

In the fall of 1981, my Mossad career ended for a second time. I finished drafting my resignation letter, placed it on Haka's desk and went to the beach.

Three months later came a phone call from Danny: "If I arrange a special contract for you, will you come?"

Never one to be daunted by directors and directives, he ignored the fact that I was out of the loop and told me what he had accomplished in the last few months.

He had set up a straw company in Europe, ostensibly focused on tourism. "We have an airplane in an African country, sort of, maintain a sumptuous office in Europe, though there is no one in it, and a large budget to get the Jews out. I recruited Jonathan and went to Sudan," he told me. "Jonathan," Danny hastened to explain, "is a former Navy SEAL and a Mossad guy with extensive operational experience, who set up a thriving security company after his departure from the civil service. We toured the coastline and found an abandoned holiday village formerly run by an Italian company.

We leased it and signed a contract with the Sudanese government to develop and promote underwater sports on the Red Sea.

"We've already used the village as a cover for one operation that can be summed up in one word: crazy. We have a wonderful crew, and against all odds we were able to rescue 164 Jews from refugee camps, transport them hundreds of kilometers to the shore and transfer them with the help of navy commandos to the Israel Navy vessel *Bat Galim*, cruising off the shoreline. Now we'd like to streamline the system and run similar operations with greater frequency. I must have someone like you on the team. I already have too many Foreign Legionnaires."

"Foreign Legionnaires?" I asked.

"Splendid people each and every one of them, but not Mossad: mechanics, driving instructors, hoteliers, doctors. They have no idea what covert operational activity is all about. They keep breaking all the rules. They are capable of going to Sudan wearing Israeli-made 'Ata' work shirts and playing audio cassettes of Shlomo Artzi [a popular Israeli singer]. It's just a matter of time before someone makes a mistake that would force us to abort the operation. There are two or three ex-Mossad employees, but they work independently now and their businesses might go under in their absence, so they can't commit themselves to long stints. This mission requires someone with experience who would go to Sudan for at least three months, check out the territory and get things ready for the upcoming operations. Are you on?"

Danny had twisted someone's arm to offer me a year's special contract, even though barely three months had elapsed since I left slamming the door behind me. The following morning I returned to work with the Mossad. May this book serve as my delayed explanation to all the regulars on the trendy Dabush beach below the Herzliya hotel strip — which then was still a small and intimate place known to real sea lovers — who wondered in the fall of 1981 where I disappeared to without bidding them farewell.

Chapter 7

The Khartoum Hilton stuck out in its splendor amidst the congestion, dust, poverty and heat surrounding it like the negative of an opulent black villa in the heart of a white desert.

The white building was planned in the United States and Europe, then transported in sections to Sudan and set up exactly at the confluence of the Blue and White Niles. From here, the river flows on, overcoming thirty-three hundred kilometers of desert land to pour into the Mediterranean. Except for the Nile water that was used in mixing the concrete, and has long since evaporated, the hotel had no local, Sudanese components whatsoever. Even the sheets and towels were imported from the United States, an economic absurdity since Sudan makes fine cotton in abundance.

"We don't take chances," one of the managers explained one day. "Our motto is total independence. We do not depend on the local electricity grid, which provides fluctuating current, and only during certain hours of the day. Water supply is also independent. The water is filtered by special devices built in the basement, and the kitchen gets its supplies regularly by air from Europe."

These facts explain why the hotel charged such high rates, in dollars, and why it was always full. There were two other hotels in Khartoum, of a reasonable level: the Meridien and the Friendship Palace, but they suffered from the hotel version of Murphy's Law: no air-conditioning one day, food poisoning afflicting the guests the following day, thefts from rooms, phones that didn't always work. And this is only a partial checklist.

No wonder, then, that before Ruby and I left for Sudan, Danny told us in no uncertain terms: "Only the Hilton; don't even bother with other hotels."

The familiar strains of *"Hava Nagila"* ("let's rejoice," a famous

Israeli song) welcomed us as we went through the rotating door, trading the sweltering air outside for the air-conditioned lobby of the Khartoum Hilton.

A couple of Hungarian musicians, a pianist and a violinist, provided musical ambiance in the bar, which boasted the romantic name Sunset. And there, thousands of miles from Budapest, it appeared that the melody to the Israeli song, complete with the strains of whining violins, was part of the Hungarian music repertoire.

Around the elegant bar, equipped with the choicest products of the alcohol distilleries of the infidel Christian world — something that marked the Hilton as a cursed place in the eyes of extremist, violent Muslims and explained the need for the permanent presence of a police patrol car in front of the hotel — were sitting several characters, the usual blend of patrons of the Khartoum Hilton.

Soon enough we came to know them.

In the center sat Billy, a plumpish American, a senior executive with the Chevron oil conglomerate. From his hotel room he accomplished the near impossible task of coordinating and supervising the activities of the company's drilling crews in southern Sudan, the heart of rebel-controlled territory. His job included overseeing supplies to the oil crew base camp a thousand kilometers south of Khartoum. His mission was facilitated by helicopters, light aircraft, numerous trucks and jeeps. The experts looking for the black gold did not lack funding. It is also conceivable that some of his oil engineers were in fact CIA agents who kept feeding Washington with updates about the goings-on in Sudan, and particularly in its unruly southern region.

There was also Jacques the Frenchman, a representative of an international aid agency, a balding, nervous man, aged about forty, who never stopped complaining. His monthly hotel bill plus the quantities of imported cognac he imbibed daily would have been enough to feed a whole refugee camp for a year.

At the far end of the bar sat Henry, a Canadian about the same age as Jacques. He stared down at a full glass of Canadian Club whiskey. Henry was working for a rival international aid outfit, but instead of cooperating with Jacques for the good of the refugees, he only tried to have his rival expelled from Sudan by getting him involved in bribery and other sleazy scams to clear the way for his group to take over.

His drinking partner was Teddy, short for Theodosius, a smooth-talking Greek, who together with his father ran a tourist-transport-contraband office in Khartoum with branches in every remote Sudanese town. Sudanese-born, the thirty-year-old was among the last members left of the international community in Khartoum from before the 1956 declaration of independence. Most foreigners had left over the years after the departure of the British, only regretting not having done so earlier. They included about a hundred Jewish families who maintained a magnificent syna-gogue in the heart of the capital, which nowadays stands locked and deserted. Life in Sudan provided a superb school for business, to wit: at least ninety of those hundred families, many of which have resettled in Geneva, Switzerland, appear on the roster of the world's richest Jews today, including Nissim Gaon, who, according to foreign press reports, continued to be involved in all kinds of business in Sudan while providing cover stories for activities to rescue Ethiopian Jews.

Teddy the Greek was a local fixer and together with a Sudanese partner, Kamal, who also visited the bar daily, was able to arrange for anything: "You need gasoline? Travel permits? A visitor's visa? Or better still a license to hunt lions in a government-run game reserve? Or maybe you'd rather hunt an elephant?"

Supporting Teddy, Kamal and hundreds of local fixers were dozens of international aid organizations, which dispatched rep-resentatives to Khartoum without any coordination among them. Had the European donors known what their money — earmarked for alleviating the suffering of millions of starving refugees — was being wasted on, they would have picked another outlet for it. But Europe is pretty distant from Sudan and the fact that only a fifth of any aid shipment from Europe finally reached the needy was something the Sunset bar dwellers could live with.

At the other end of the well-kept bar sat Said, an ageless Palestinian, one of the Palestine Liberation Organization envoys in Khartoum. He guzzled PLO money received from the Gulf States by downing countless glasses of Chivas Regal, interspersed with occasional swigs of Karkade, a local hibiscus leaf drink served hot or cold. Another version of the drink is called Nous-Nous, meaning half and half (half lemonade and half Karkade).

His drinking partner was another Palestinian whose job was to arrange orgies for a well-heeled Saudi prince, who, for reasons known only to himself, used to hop over from Riyadh to Khartoum for a hot night in the hotel's royal suite with top local prostitutes.

And there were senior Sudanese officials, airline crews and businessmen from all over the world who were eager to land some particularly lucrative deal financed by the World Bank, Arab Bank or any other international organization with huge sums of money and minimal control apparatus.

Rounding out the Sunset bar population were at least three Mossad men: Ruby, myself and someone else.

We were not the only Mossad agents working in Sudan. "In addition to your operation, aimed at extricating hundreds of Jews at one go," we were told at our pre-departure briefing, "we have another operation running, sending small groups of Jews from Sudan to Europe."

It was further explained to us that an international aid outfit had been convinced to cooperate with the State of Israel to rescue refugees of war and hunger from Africa. The fact that they were Jews did not concern the heads of that organization. All they wanted was to save souls from disease and hunger, whoever they were. No one needed to know that those refugees would not remain in Europe but would proceed in various ways to Israel.

"Even if you identify one of our people," admonished the briefing officers before we headed out, "ignore them. Not a wink or a raised eyebrow. Nada."

The moment I sat at the bar, I recognized the head of the unit engaged in flying refugees from Khartoum — a Mossad veteran, with countless operations in every part of the world under his belt. Several years earlier we happened to work together. Now he was sitting on a bar stool, five meters away from me, one hand clasping a cold glass of beer, and the other alternating between stuffing his pipe with tobacco and turning pages of a spy novel.

We ignored each other like a hotheaded couple after a particularly stormy fight. Nothing. Zero. Air.

Moments later, in our sumptuous room overlooking the hotel swimming pool, after turning up the sound on the radio to drown out our voices, I updated Ruby about the identity of the pipe-stuffing individual.

"You know each other and you didn't even say 'Shalom'? How does he manage to keep his sanity in this place?" wondered Ruby. "Alone, absolutely alone, fake identity, no friends, no help. What a guy."

Chapter 8

A day in Sudan has twenty-four hours, but time there has a completely different meaning than in the West.

"The car will be ready tomorrow," Hassan, the Tourism Authority representative, promised day in and day out. But despite the promises, always accompanied by a trust-building sweep of the hand in the direction of the heart, many "tomorrows" had passed before we could get ourselves together for a trip to "our" holiday village — traveling over a twelve-hundred-kilometer (750-mile) road. This was Sudan's only paved road, and nowhere along the route is there a gas station, a garage or a decent hotel.

One day, under pressure from headquarters for us to get to the beach without delay, Ruby and I decided to step up the preparations. We heard that at a military camp at the edge of Khartoum it was possible to purchase, with an appropriate bribe, full oil drums at a price that would not incite the Mossad accountants to riot.

For twenty Sudanese pounds — about fifteen US dollars, a small fortune in local terms — the owner of an aged yellow Hillman Hunter taxi agreed to take us around the city to see the sights and remain available to us for the rest of the day. He proudly pointed out colonial buildings built by the Turks in the 1820s bordering on the broad Sharia el Nile Boulevard, adorned with wide-canopied trees, which draw their water directly from the muddy Nile waters flowing on the other side. Among the buildings were small palaces, including the governor's house, now used by Nimeiri, and the historic Grand Hotel, which was built at the turn of the century by the Germans and once played host to Menachem Begin on his historic trip to South Africa. But it had been completely eclipsed by the recent addition of the Hilton.

Khartoum is a relatively new city. Tutti Island, which overlooks the confluence point of the White and the Blue Niles, has remains of ancient habitation, but the beginnings of Khartoum as a city go back to a trading post built by the Turks in the 1820s. The British, who arrived in Sudan as partners of the Egyptians and the Turks, expanded the town along European lines, including a low perimeter wall and straight, intersecting streets.

No trace was left of Old Khartoum. At the end of the nineteenth century a local ruler, the Mahdi, rebelled against the British rulers, slaughtered all the foreigners, including the governor general "China" Gordon, and wiped Khartoum off the face of the earth. In its place, the Mahdi established his capital Omdurman on the west bank of the Nile. Only in 1898 did General Kitchener raise the Union Jack again over Khartoum, after using machine-gun fire to rout the Mahdi's lance-wielding cavalry, in a battle attended by a young journalist named Winston Churchill, who of course did his best to laud this victory.

From the start of the twentieth century large British investments were made in Sudan. The capital, Khartoum, was rebuilt as a cluster of cities, also comprising Khartoum North and Omdurman. Government and educational institutions were established, including a university, hospitals, mosques and temples for all denominations. The Catholic Church there was endowed by the Austrian Kaiser Franz Josef, for no apparent reason. An industrial infrastructure was developed, including a dockyard for river boats, textile and food processing plants, an electricity grid for public transport and a large railroad complex, including a terminal and maintenance facilities for the busiest train system in Africa.

According to Jews who lived in British Khartoum, the city was peaceful and sleepy, baked in the heat, but quiet and well run.

Soon after independence in 1956, Khartoum changed. Millions of villagers flocked there in search of employment — a typical phenomenon in Third World countries — causing it to choke for lack of adequate infrastructure. When Ruby and I arrived in Khartoum at the end of 1981 there were no longer any street cars. In fact, they had ground to a halt in the 1960s because of maintenance problems. The sewage and electricity supply systems had collapsed, and telephones worked haphazardly.

Our aged Hillman Hunter withstood the difficult road conditions — deep potholes and large rocks used by drivers to prop up their tire jacks after their vehicles broke down and then left in the road — which would have caused any other European-made car to fall apart. There were also huge puddles of sewage water. The driver, a happy Sudanese in a typical wide, white robe and a huge turban made of a sparkling white kerchief looped around his head, gave us a free demonstration of Khartoum-style gas conservation driving. The moment the car reached forty kilometers (twenty-five miles) an hour he geared down to neutral and rode the downgrades with the engine switched completely off, relying solely on Sir Isaac Newton's force of gravity.

We drove by gas stations besieged by hundreds of taxicabs and private cars whose drivers had been waiting patiently for fresh fuel supplies to be delivered. According to our guide, sometimes three days went by before a double miracle occurred: the delivery of gas supplies and the resumption of electricity so the pumps could work and enable each driver to receive his weekly ration of ten liters of gasoline.

Our visit to the military base was a total failure. We joined hundreds of nervous Sudanese, many of them fixers with ample contacts, who ringed an office inside a small structure from where the fuel allocation clerk operated. Shoving and being "polite" white people saying, "Sorry, may we get by" in a fake British accent brought us soon enough to the front of the line, but we came nowhere near to enlarging our gasoline stocks.

"Sorry," said the army clerk. "It's no longer a matter of money. We simply ran out of gas. The tanks are empty. We know that tomorrow a tanker should be arriving at Port Sudan from Jeddah with several thousand tons, a gift of the Saudi Arabian government. But it will take at least another week before the gas gets here."

A check back with the hotel bore out the clerk's information, which I shared with a couple of young German tourists, who sat dejected in the shade of one of the structures.

Their Land Rover had died, its tank as parched as the desert. Local hustlers took money from them promising to provide some gas and disappeared. In short, in a rundown army base on the edge of Khartoum the Germans learned the hard way that they had to do their homework before setting out on an adventurous trip crossing Africa from north to south. "There's no chance to find gas here," I told them. "Go to the German embassy, they must have an emergency depot of several thousand liters. At worst, they will be able to at least help you get home safely."

While Ruby and I were drying up at the military base, our friend Hassan managed to get his hands on a single barrel of fuel. "Super quality, clean, decent price," he said naming a figure that made us whistle in protest. We could judge from the smell that it was gasoline indeed, though of dubious octane level. Car engines in Sudan tolerated anything as long as the dirty texture did not become so viscous it made them stall.

Did we have a choice? We bought the barrel from him and gave him an extra bonus.

In the afternoon, we hopped over to the management of the Tourist Corporation, the government company Danny had rented the holiday village from, and which according to the leasing agreement was our managing partner.

The doorman, who is supposed to screen the stream of visitors, had been at his shift for hours, but was still alert as we walked through the portals of the office. He must not have seen a tourist with any promise for a long time and led us directly to the general manager's office. The general manager was happy to see two "serious" businesspeople who had come to Sudan to put the country on the international tourist map and further advance his own career.

The huge ceiling fan rotated slowly, just like the flies whose movement appeared to be hampered by the heat. The new and amiable manager appeared eager to cooperate, and hopefully take his share of future profits. Ruby and I spun imaginary tales about the feverish activity conducted by our people in Europe that would soon translate into hordes of well-heeled divers swarming Sudanese diving sites in the Red Sea.

The Sudanese are extremely hospitable, despite their tough life, and therefore we drank a lot of tea before we could take leave of all the clerks and managers. The manager was greatly impressed with us and our descriptions, and when we wanted to go, begging off with "we have a lot of urgent business and many things to take care of," he proudly showed us, as if unveiling a small treasure, a supply of sheets and blankets intended for our holiday village. They had not been unpacked since the Italian entrepreneurs who built the village had left Sudan in the mid-1970s without commencing operations.

The manager was happy to transfer responsibility for this important government property over to us, even though he didn't appear to have much else to do. In return for a scrawl on some official form he gladly turned over his cache, so vital for promoting tourism to Sudan. Considering the workload of this particular government office, it would not surprise me if the form I signed is still lurking in an empty file in some cabinet in the manager's office.

Chapter 9

We spent New Year's Eve and January 1, 1982, which is Sudan's Independence Day, in Khartoum waiting for word from Hassan that our car, an International Scout that Danny had managed to buy on a previous tour, was ready to hit the road. Because the New Year happened to fall on a Thursday and everything was closed in Khartoum, we used the time for sunbathing at the hotel's handsome pool. It was the time before anyone knew about the hole in the ozone layer and the dangers of bronzing oneself. Around the pool, in a perfect holiday atmosphere, lounged diplomats' families, well-heeled Sudanese, as well as pretty air hostesses from Alitalia and beefy ones from several Arab airlines.

Unlike the detailed descriptions in Hollywood spy novels, Ruby and I refrained from any romantic forays. Not that we weren't interested, but we were concerned that our cover stories would be compromised. Ruby, an ex-kibbutznik, amateur oboe player, and a former Navy SEAL, did speak fluent English, with a noticeable Israeli accent, but any link between him and the passport he carried was purely coincidental. And even I, whose accent was far better than his, decided to give up on casual flirtations so as not to put the operation in peril. We therefore used our free time pounding the pavement throughout Khartoum.

At the main junction of Jamaah and Kasr streets, a poor, lone policeman was making efforts to control traffic streaming furiously from the train station towards the Unity Monument and the presidential palace. There were many carts, countless Toyota Hilux pickup trucks, which have successfully replaced the camel throughout the Arab world, and several camels taken by Bedouin to be slaughtered.

The most useful vehicle in Sudan is a light truck, usually a 1950s vintage Bedford, which due to the heavy demand in the Sudanese market was still being manufactured in England at a limited assembly line. The trucks reach Sudan fitted only with an engine and a steering wheel. Their chassis is embellished by local artisans with a sumptuous structure — there is a spacious cabin with open holes for doors and windows that provides space for the driver and up to six passengers, and a tall box for cargo. In front, the truck has regular tires, but the rear axle has two larger tires, to improve its ability to cope with obstacles on the road. Each truck's team included a driver and an assistant whose job is to collect the fares, refuel the truck from oil drums in the cargo box and also remain watchful for any mechanical problem when the vehicle gets bogged down in the middle of the desert.

In the absence of any transport infrastructure, these trucks carry the entire burden of commercial activity for this huge country. "In Sudan, a mechanical device requiring any maintenance tools beyond a five-kilo hammer and a simple soldering iron is headed for breakdown in no time," Billy, the American Chevron coordinator, explained to me. "The Bedford trucks are simply indestructible. They just go, go, and go."

In our long months in Sudan we learned to appreciate the driving and improvisational skills of the Sudanese truck drivers. The terrain they covered would be considered by any Israeli military intelligence office as impassable except by tanks. The fact that often the trucks move with torn tires, broken suspension, and engines held together with steel wire doesn't bother the locals at all — as long as the horn works, the engine rattles and the vehicle trundles along.

In the city's markets, through the constant cloud rising from the dusty street, a Western visitor receives an introductory lesson in Africanology. Some three hundred kilometers (185 miles) from Khartoum, international aid organizations are fighting famine. On the other hand, in Khartoum, the markets are overflowing with plenty — heaps of fresh vegetables, small lemons, corn, peanuts in endless supply (called *ful Sudani* in Arabic), and mammoth quantities of meat, topped with swarms of flies.

In short, the basic problem relating to famine is therefore not lack of food but its mode of storage and distribution to the hungry. With the absence of storage and distribution facilities, famine lurks, and will break out whenever the political or demographic balance in areas farther from the capital is disrupted.

The pungent smell of spiced meat rose from one of the stalls in the street. And after a week of ingesting highly expensive European food in the Hilton restaurants, I felt like sampling some local stuff. I used to be known to my colleagues at work as "iron stomach" because of the culinary experiments I put my digestive system through in exotic places. I proceeded on the assumption that as someone born in the 1950s — the years of economic austerity in Israel when Kupat Holim, the national health service, pumped newborns with huge quantities of penicillin — my body could stand up to such torture.

The stall owner, glad of an opportunity to acquaint a European guest with his delicacies, suggested I try a kebab made of camel meat and mutton, immersed in *Um Riggaya*, a tomato and okra sauce. It was tasty and apparently not too contaminated, since I survived to tell you about it. This whole meal set me back half a guinea (i.e., half a Sudanese pound), a distant relative of the English guinea, which equaled one pound and one shilling and harks back to a gold pound issued in the African state of Guinea.

Overjoyed by the lip-smacking noises made by his patron, the vendor suggested that we round off the culinary feast with *Arageh*, local araq made of dates. The opaque glass bottle in which it came had been used, in my opinion, by General Kichener's troops in the previous century. I decided that this would be too much, so I passed.

There were strange activities in the shade of the colonial edifices in the city center that might make a visitor think that Sudan is an African version of Switzerland. There were dozens of watch repair stalls. The watchmakers would open up the timepieces while wearing a loupe, rummage through the insides with thin blade screwdrivers, spray them and return the watch to the client, contented that the hands on his timepiece had started moving again, albeit without any direction or rhythm, and all this in return for a few pennies.

Business goes on concurrently on the streets and in shops. In the more elegant ones, few and far between, aged air conditioners strain to relieve the heat. Souvenir shops use hawkers to hustle the white people into their stores, crammed to the ceiling with tiger skins, tons of ivory in every shape and form, drums, wooden sculptures and numerous other items, mostly banned from trading. Despite the proximity to the equator, the business protocol draws on Middle Eastern traditions: the vendor names a very high sum, saying, "Believe me, I'm making you a very special price," which eventually decreases to a level that reflects the buyer's bargaining skills. Since tourism isn't exactly a booming business in Khartoum, the souvenir vendors make most of their money from trading in foreign currency at rates far superior to the official ones.

Most Khartoum residents are Muslims who regard themselves as part of the Arab world. Many of them, black and tall, fit the collective image of Sudanese soldiers as remembered by Israeli troops who besieged an Egyptian battalion in which the Sudanese were serving in the "Falouja Pocket," an Egyptian enclave in the Negev desert, during the Israeli Independence War in 1948–49.

Their traditional garb includes a white cotton tunic and a long, white scarf tied around the head like a turban. A casual stroll through the streets of the capital reveals the presence of black Christian Sudanese from the southern part of the country.

In the early 1980s, before fundamentalist Islam took over, one could see Catholic nuns talking amicably with female Muslim students, their eyes peering through veils, and women dressed in quasi Western clothes. Each time I returned to Sudan I noticed an increase in the number of veiled women in the streets, a firm testimonial to the success of the fundamentalist takeover in Sudanese society.

Chapter 10

In the first week of January 1982, Ruby and I left Khartoum heading south to "our" holiday village in the Port Sudan area along the Red Sea coast. As the crow flies, Khartoum lies some five hundred kilometers (about three hundred miles) from the Red Sea. But in order to encourage the development of the eastern sector of Sudan, the only road linking Khartoum to the country's sole seaport was built in a semicircle. You drive south, then east, and after some twelve hundred taxing kilometers (750 miles) of driving — something like driving from the northern tip of Israel to the southern end and back again — reach your destination.

The American jeep started the ride at a pleasant trot, perhaps because of the landscape, which reminded it of its homeland, Texas. On the left, the Nile flowed languidly. On the right stretched fields of cotton, sorghum and other crops, with irrigation channels extending to the yellow horizon, which marks the beginning of the desert that ends thousands of kilometers to the west, on the other side of the African continent.

After a tranquil hour's drive, as we were getting close to Hasaisa village, only a hundred kilometers (sixty miles) from Khartoum, the engine suddenly began producing weird noises, the temperature gauge shot up and the engine stalled.

"Maybe the jeep got road weary," Ruby quipped. "It suddenly dawned on it that this was not America and that between Khartoum and Port Sudan there is no mechanic that could tend to it."

Our combined mechanical knowledge was enough for both of us to concur that the problem was very serious indeed. Dozens of Sudanese drivers promptly stopped to graciously offer help. But they too threw their hands up in the air after studying the sophis-

ticated entrails of the strange vehicle, so much different from the
basic engines that power the common transport in Sudan.

We improvised a makeshift cooling device for the engine, and
turned back. With Ruby at the wheel, I squirted water into the
engine every thirty seconds. This contrivance took us fifty kilometers on our way back toward Khartoum and the air-conditioned
Hilton Hotel. And then the engine conked out for good. The combination of Sudanese terrain and fatal Israeli ingenuity apparently
proved too much for the jeep.

Salvation came in the form of a smiling Sudanese who owned a
Toyota Hilux pickup truck. Fifty guineas, which to him was a small
fortune, persuaded him to tow us to Khartoum. The fact that the
heavy and overloaded jeep nearly caused his truck to break in two
did not bother him. He apparently figured he could take his truck
to a blacksmith for repairs, and what mattered was being able to
help two strangers get home, not to mention the tidy sum he'd
make in the process.

News of our return to Khartoum raised a ruckus in Tel Aviv
headquarters. They had planned another rescue operation for
January, and it now seemed that the timetable was going awry.

We impressed on headquarters that the problem was serious
and that a way out had to be found.

"There's no choice. You've got to move," they said, forgetting
the hackneyed Arab proverb "haste comes from the devil." "In your
hotel lives another one of our men who deals with taking Jews
to Europe with the help of international aid groups. He has been
ordered to give you his Toyota, so you can hit the road immediately.
Since there is operational risk involved in meeting him openly, do
it speedily and carefully."

Going against the ground edicts of covert activity, and breaking every compartmentalization rule, we met the car owner. In
the gated parking lot at the back of the hotel, we identified a tall
young man we had bumped into in the corridors and elevators, not
suspecting for one moment that he was part of our forces.

Later on, in Sudan when our paths crossed again, it turned out that despite his young looks, he had managed to graduate from medical school in Jerusalem, and due to his perfect command of English, and other personal qualities, was recruited for "temporary work" in Sudan. We greeted each other with a curt "*Shalom.*" "My name is Dr. Shlomo Pomeranz," he whispered with a smile. We shook hands and received the car keys and papers.

"I had some security problems with the vehicle," he managed to say before going away. "Make sure you are updated by headquarters."

A "security problem" refers to any minor incident that could expose covert activity. Headquarters did send us an update: "On your way to Port Sudan don't stop at the checkpoint at the entrance to Gedaref. This vehicle has seen a lot of activity in the area in recent months, and might cause you to be suspected by police. Good luck."

Chapter 11

The following morning, at dawn, we took leave of civilization at the Hilton and hit the road again in our new Toyota, a massive jeep-pickup truck for three, adapted to driving in Sudan's difficult terrain, and whose dashboard had far fewer switches than the more sophisticated International Scout vehicle that had failed us.

The greatest advantage of the Toyota was the contraption added to it locally: a large, cage-like cargo box, the creation of a local blacksmith, which secured our equipment from greedy hands. We placed our equipment in the lockable cage: a barrel of gasoline, oil cans, well-disguised communication gear, diversified diving gear, sleeping bags, crates of food and drink, and the Tourist Corporation package of sheets and blankets.

An hour later we went past Hasaisa, where our previous attempt at the journey had been aborted. A large group of prisoners in tatters, bound to each other in chains, were digging a trench parallel to the road. Sleepy policemen, armed with ancient British rifles, kept watch.

"That's how we'll look if they catch us," Ruby reflected out loud.

"Mommy told me not to go on this trip," I answered jokingly, stepping on the accelerator even harder.

The Toyota covered the road effortlessly. The road was in relatively good condition, with few potholes and light traffic, mostly trucks and buses. From time to time, improvised rock barricades appeared across the road. "In Sudan there are no warning triangles," explained Ruby, who had taken part in the first operation in the fall. "A driver who gets stuck at night builds a small barricade of rocks about one hundred meters ahead of and behind the vehicle, both as a warning and to shield the vehicle from being hit. When the problem is fixed, the rocks remain in the road until the local public works department embarks on a road-clearing campaign. But such a campaign takes place only once every few weeks, and in the meantime the road gets covered with rocks. You have no idea how dangerous it is to drive at night, particularly when you are half asleep…"

Another hour of driving south brought us to a junction several kilometers north of Wad Madani, the most modern city in Sudan, and a large industrial and agricultural center.

We turned left, due east. At the junction itself, like others across the country, we came upon an army and police checkpoint. Oil drums reinforced with rocks served as a barrier. The policemen were amiable, peeked inside, asked, "Where to?" took a small transit fee and sent us on our way with a handshake and a blessing.

The landscape changed abruptly. Desert from horizon to horizon, devoid of human beings. The morning coolness had long disappeared. It was getting hot inside the Toyota, and our bladders sent distress signals.

We decided to stop for a tea break. Since we had been warned not to stop at Gedaref, we parked in a small village called Kheir, about a hundred kilometers before Gedaref. A "village" was an overstatement as far as a place like Kheir goes. It is no more than an assortment of tin and straw cabins, located along the main road, some serving as "thousand-star" inns (thus called for the stars peeking through the broken roof), and others offering weary motorists hot tea, cold drinks (which are hot as well, in the absence of electricity to operate the fridge), and local food.

As we were sipping our teas lazily, we noticed a policeman standing by the Toyota. The policeman, a broad-shouldered man aged about forty, examined the Toyota from every possible angle. He went around it once, and twice and then with jerky hand movements, called out to his buddies in a strained voice.

"What's the matter with him?" wondered Ruby aloud, and before he was able to complete the sentence, the policeman parked himself in front of us. We raised our eyes from the steaming teacups and found ourselves staring into the muzzle of a British rifle — the unsafe end — held in the shaking hands of an anxious policeman. He was not alone. Next to him were two civilians in white shirts, one of them brandishing a black handgun, also British-made.

"Show us your papers right away," one of the civilians ordered in Arabic.

"English. Do you speak English?" we replied with feigned indifference and the realization that something had gone awfully wrong. "Papers, fast," said the civilian, who by now appeared to have been infected by the policeman's nervousness, and switched his handgun from hand to hand.

The handgun was a bit rusty, and the rifle too looked like a museum piece, but we had no intention of finding out if they worked for real.

"There's something wrong here," I answered calmly. "Please, here are our papers. We are Tourist Corporation employees going to Port Sudan."

The image of the chained prisoners at Hasaisa flashed immediately before my eyes. Ruby confided later that he too had the same vision.

The civilian did not bother answering. He took the passports, told the policeman to watch us, and disappeared into a tin shack that appeared to be in better shape than the others.

With racing pulses, but outwardly staying calm, we continued drinking our teas. Minutes later, the civilian returned, accompanied by a young assistant.

"Go to Gedaref, you drive," he told us, pointing at our Toyota. We got into the vehicle; I slid into the driver's seat, Ruby sat next to me and the young assistant, his pistol drawn, sat by the right-hand door. The policeman who had started the whole incident sat in the cage in the back.

Chapter 12

The trip to Gedaref lasted more than an hour. A long and unpleasant hour. Our guard was bent on wearing a tough expression. Our attempts to strike a conversation hit a wall of silence. The only words he uttered were "thank you" when he was offered a cigarette.

Ruby and I continued to play the parts of innocent, uncomprehending strangers. We were talking to each other in English, occasionally injecting verbal provocations, such as "he has a urine stain on his pants," to check his reaction. There was none. He either was an accomplished actor or truly understood no word of English. But Ruby and I took no chances, and continued to play innocent until we reached the local Sudanese security forces headquarters at the entrance to Gedaref.

The Toyota entered a large complex through a gate in a low white brick wall. In the center there was a pitiful parade ground, with remnants of whitewash and a flagpole flying a tattered Sudanese flag. There were a few elongated structures, reminiscent of the old barracks at Israel's Tel Hashomer Army Base built in central Israel under the British Mandate, an apparent British hand-me-down. Policemen and civilians were slumped in small groups under two trees that had managed to strike root in the loose sand.

We pulled up in front of the main building, a long, narrow hut. I pointed out to myself that the antenna on the roof was broken and rusty, something that would indicate that communications at the place had been out of commission for years. The policeman remained on guard, and the young civilian, holding our passports, went inside.

Minutes later, he reappeared in the company of an officer, and read out Ruby's name from his passport.

I made a quick assessment of the situation. I considered that we were not at war now, but on a secret mission, and also that we had not been taken prisoner, but were "merely" under interrogation to clarify some particulars. For some reason, we were under suspicion. Why, exactly, I did not know. For the present, we were being treated well, and it could all prove to be a mistake. Therefore, I, not Ruby, should be questioned, since I had a better cover story and had undergone training on how to handle such situations.

I signaled to Ruby to stay put, and went into the hut.

I was shown into a room that at first glance reminded me of an image from an old copy of the Israeli army weekly magazine *Bamahane* — an Israeli army battalion commander's office in the 1950s. But Nimeiri's photo on the wall reminded me we were in Sudan. A fan covered with cobwebs hung from the ceiling. Natural light trickled in from two small windows. There was no electrical light, indicating that electricity was out as well. I told myself that this was the only bright spot in our situation.

A dark-skinned officer with handsome features, except for a few scars along his cheek, typical of some Sudanese tribes, sat behind a desk on a leather armchair. It was an ornate piece of furniture, à la Louis XIV.

Our passports were placed on the desk. Behind it stood a young army captain. A policeman stood at attention by the door. On a small stand were several telephones in different colors; when I moved toward him to shake his hand, as if this were a routine visit, I noticed that they were covered with dust.

He did not offer his hand nor stand up, but said calmly — too calmly for my taste — "Sit down," pointing at a simple wooden chair.

I sat down. The officer opened the top passport, which was Ruby's, compared the picture to the person sitting in front of him, laid it down and took mine.

Despite his heavy accent, his English was superb, fluent and rich. He shot out his questions in a rapid staccato. "Who are you, what are you, where are you going, when did you arrive in Sudan, where do you live?" He was not satisfied with the city I mentioned, but also demanded to know the street name and the house number, comparing it with my driver's permit, which had been impounded at the Kheir checkpoint.

I answered naturally, in a pretty jubilant voice, and right after he fired off his second question, I injected questions of my own: "Did something happen, and why are two loyal Tourist Corporation workers heading for their workplace taken under guard to a police station?"

He did not bother answering and continued asking questions which soon enough became more and more personal: "Why do you work in Sudan, not in Europe, how did you get this job, who approached you, and where?" Some of the questions were repeated in several versions — a well-known tactic of any novice interrogator, which is designed to cross-reference between the suspect's answers and pinpoint inconsistencies and contradictions. At this point, I was already sweating like a marathon runner in mid-race. "It's hot here, may I have something to drink?" I asked the officer, who I only now noticed had the rank of a colonel. "I think I deserve an answer, and what do you want of us anyway?"

No drink, nor answer. The interrogator started consulting with the young captain. They were talking in a Khartoum dialect, very similar to the Egyptian one. How grateful I was then for every second of alertness that enabled me to absorb something of Mr. Mizrahi's lessons at the Shabak domestic security service crash Arabic course. I didn't understand all of their conversation, but nevertheless formed a picture in my mind.

The policeman who saw us at the Kheir tea house identified the Toyota by color and shape and even two digits from the license plate. According to his account, two weeks earlier, a white man drove up to the Kheir checkpoint. It was late at night, and disobeying orders to stop, the driver increased his speed, ran off the road to get around the barrier, and continued galloping into the desert. The soldiers manning the roadblock, convinced that they were facing gun or drug runners, responded with heavy fire from their Kalashnikov assault rifles.

The new piece of information made me furious at our headquarters, not at the Sudanese. So this was the "security trouble" we were told about — a shooting incident, no less. And it did not happen at Gedaref, as we were told, but at Kheir, where we had stopped off in order to avoid possible trouble in Gedaref.

Outwardly, I remained calm, although by this time I had become truly worried. The interrogation went on. There were more questions, now focusing on the vehicle. "Whose is it, how long have you had it, were you ever in the Gedaref area?" All the answers were duly supplied in full. Luckily for me, the two men frequently consulted each other in Arabic, so I knew more or less what the next question would be.

Meanwhile, a light began flickering at the end of the interrogation tunnel. "If the antenna on the roof of the shack is broken, the phones are covered with a layer of dust and no electrical bulb is burning," I thought to myself, "then they have no communications with Khartoum, or else they would have called up their headquarters and the Hilton Hotel itself to verify the information I have given them."

"Gentlemen," I told them, "I demand to know what you suspect us of. With one telephone call you can obtain all the details you want from the Hilton. I don't understand why you are asking so many questions about our poor pickup truck, which must be brought to Port Sudan today."

At this stage, the interrogators were beginning to experience doubt. All of a sudden, they stopped being tough, ordered one of the soldiers to fetch me a glass of tea and started asking general questions. The young officer also told the sentry to look for the policeman who identified us in Kheir leading to our detention.

Sipping sweetened tea, I heard the policeman giving his account of the incident to the officers. I could hardly suppress a smile when he described in a loud voice how he had fired at the truck. "I sprayed the Toyota from a distance of up to ten meters," he said enthusiastically, carried on the wings of Middle Eastern fantasy. He added another sentence that in retrospect led to our being freed: "I emptied another clip and saw dozens of bullets hitting the Toyota."

"That's it, we're off the hook," I thought with relief. Now the officers would examine the Toyota, and as I had finished loading it up only several hours earlier I knew the body showed no suspect bullet holes. I have no doubt the Sudanese did shoot in the direction of the Toyota, but evidently his marksmanship was very poor as there was no logical explanation for his inability to hit the vehicle even once.

"Come with us," they told me. "We want you to unload all the equipment in the truck."

Ruby heaved a sigh of relief when he saw me emerging from the shack after two hours of interrogation, smiling and in one piece.

"What's the matter?" he asked in a soft voice.

"I think it's going to be alright," I whispered. "It'll soon be over."

Aided by two soldiers and under the watchful gaze of the officers, the cargo was unloaded. The policemen checked every centimeter of the Toyota, crawled under it and found no trace of the dozens of bullets that had ostensibly pierced its metal shell. The colonel audibly reprimanded the policeman, and the captain added a juicy swearword which was received with ripples of laughter by the other policemen and comments about the wild imagination of the shooter. He attempted to explain, but was silenced by the colonel barking, "Enough of your thousand-and-one-nights tales."

With Ruby busy supervising the reloading, the two officers invited me for a toast over a glass of whiskey which produced a joint declaration of friendship and a generous invitation from me, along the lines of, "Hop over to visit the village when you have a chance — everything on us."

The moment the Toyota's wheels left the compound, Ruby started asking myriad questions. I told him about the policeman's account.

"The bastards at headquarters should go to hell for landing us in this trap," he said, adding that as the interrogation dragged on, he had already planned to use the policemen's drowsiness to escape into the desert.

After a strenuous ten-hour drive we reached Port Sudan that same evening. From the road, I sent a brief update to headquarters, including a very tame description of the detention and the incident. I figured that too detailed a description would prompt them to decide to abort the mission. Ruby and I believed that since we had emerged from the interrogation without a blemish, there was no need to cause panic at home.

Two weeks later, when Danny joined us, I gave him the full version. "You did good," he said. "Things here on the ground are never understood by those who are far away." He then told us that in the long months he had spent in Sudan he learned not to acknowledge messages that appeared to him redundant. "As long as I don't confirm, I can continue operating using my judgment and the conditions in the field," he said.

I reminded him of the story of Nelson, the one-eyed English admiral, who during one of his battles ignored an order that he didn't approve of, to break contact. "I can see no retreat flag," he said, pressing the telescope into his dead eye. He continued fighting until the battle was concluded with a British naval victory.

"Yes, indeed," Danny laughed. "We too have such a telescope."

Chapter 13

Ruby and I spent the night in the Red Sea Hotel, Port Sudan's best. Should Hollywood need a set for shooting a colonial era film, this is the place. The hotel, run by the Government Tourist Corporation, looks ready for the return of the British clerks at any minute. Three stories in all, the first floor featured a spacious smoking room with armchairs upholstered in floral fabrics that had seen better days. A large swordfish was pinned on an elegant wooden board, overlooking the entrance, topping a long roster of "Port Sudan Ace Anglers," all British officers, who had established the rule of the crown at the end of the previous century, and among other things went fishing. The last entry was from 1956.

The dining hall served English tea and biscuits in the afternoon. The rooms were spacious and clean, equipped with ceiling fans, which are vital for guests' well-being. Unlike Khartoum, which enjoys a dry climate, Port Sudan suffers from sweltering humidity. Luckily for its residents, the local power company here was far more efficient than its counterpart in the capital. Surprisingly, every room had running water in the shower and lavatories. In the yard there was an ancient waterless swimming pool. The windows on the top floors looked out on the harbor, which appeared to be a beehive of activity, bustling with boats, huge cranes and trucks.

Port Sudan was built by the British at the beginning of the twentieth century as a gateway to Sudan. It used a natural lagoon that was expanded to accommodate modern ships. The rise of Port Sudan heralded the decline of the traditional port cities along the coastline, like Suakin, a few kilometers to the south, which became a beautiful ghost city.

Officially some hundred thousand people lived in Port Sudan, but effectively the figure was much higher, swollen by a daily influx of farmers and Bedouin in search of work.

All traffic of commercial goods, except for smaller cargos hauled along the Nile from Egypt, goes through Port Sudan. Until the construction of the road we were traveling on, which was completed in the 1970s, this traffic moved on a railroad laid by the British, which linked the port with Khartoum and other parts of the country. The railroad route was shorter by one half than the modern highway to Khartoum, since the British built the track through the mountains and straight to the town of Atbara, and thence to Khartoum. Once the highway was completed, the train service was replaced by heavy trucks. The trucks, mostly antiquated Fiats donated to Sudan by Italy, massed in a huge lot at the entrance to the city. The lot was black with oil stains dripped over the years from poorly maintained trucks.

The distance to Khartoum was covered by these trucks in three days at slow speed. In Sudan there is no concept of an overload. The only test of loading capacity is the moment when the axles break down under the weight. An average heavy truck in Sudan looks like a safety inspector's nightmare: thousands of sacks of flour heaped in the box and on its trailer; atop the sacks a pickup truck is tied down, and on the heavily loaded trailer, a small private car. Thus the pickup and car owners save the gas and travel costs of the trip from Port Sudan to Khartoum. All in all, a truck would have three strata of cargo plus dozens of passengers sitting atop the flour bags. The wealthier among them were assigned, for an extra fee, an upholstered seat in the pickup truck cabin or inside the private car atop the pickup's cargo box.

A refinery was built in the 1970s by the Shell Oil Company at the south end of the city. The plant operated haphazardly, being entirely dependent on occasional crude oil shipments which the kingdom of Saudi Arabia condescended to donate to impoverished Sudan, on the other coast of the Red Sea. The city center looked just like the descriptions of the Austrian diver Hans Haas who visited Port Sudan in 1947 and was the first to photograph the amazing coral reefs in the region. He described his impressions in his book *Under the Red Sea*: "Straight streets with spacious two-story stone houses, the roofed first floor offering welcome shade." Most of the stores were owned by Indians who reached the city during the British era.

"It's a pity the British left," an Indian merchant told me a few months later. He had won our trust after managing to acquire some very rare spare parts for us several times. "Since the Union Jack was last lowered, the situation has only deteriorated. Every year, it's getting worse."

The shops at Port Sudan had a greater selection than in Khartoum, but they were characterized by the coincidental, sudden appearance of some items in many stores and the mysterious disappearance of others. The holds of the ships calling at the harbor were the source of supplies. The merchant's bargaining skills determined what the captain would be willing to part with.

At every visit to the Indian's shop, we found different items on the shelves. French cheeses made room quickly for smoked fish from Russia. German Beck's beer was replaced by San Miguel from the Philippines. One day the shop would fill up with crates of Kellogg's cereals, and the following week with Austrian alpine suntan oil. To this day, I don't know where in this furnace-like port city the Indian merchant was hoping to find potential customers for oil intended for tourists in the alpine ski resorts.

There were a few dozen Europeans in the city, mostly from Eastern Europe, but along with a smattering of Americans and British, oil and mining company representatives and envoys of various international aid groups, Korea had a significant presence in the foreigners' community because of a large tire plant they wanted to set up in the city. The Koreans lived separately in a housing compound on the outskirts of the city which, according to rumors, was the most organized and orderly place in this part of the world, a tribute to Korean diligence and self-discipline.

Chapter 14

In the early morning hours we were awakened by the shrill cries of the pampered black crows who had picked the empty lot in front of the hotel as a staging area.

After a decent breakfast we left to complete our first mission in Sudan: to reach our holiday village in peace — an additional forty-kilometer ride. We drove through an area of huge grain silos in the north of the city, where hundreds of workers were engaged in the debilitating job of loading heavy wheat sacks, bearing the inscription "Gift from the European Market." The wheat was intended for the many refugees flowing into the country, but some army trucks parked nearby indicated that the military commanders of the Port Sudan district were not oblivious to Napoleon's adage "The army marches on its stomach." In the absence of regular supplies from headquarters in Khartoum, they took care to replenish their grain stocks, at no cost to themselves, of course.

The roads inside Port Sudan were pockmarked like a moon-scape, some still wearing a thin layer of asphalt, right up to the last warehouse. A small, derelict army encampment stuck in the middle of a plain of sand and mud and a small rusty sign, directing travelers north towards the Egyptian border and the beginning of hundreds of square kilometers of sand and desolation, marked the end of civilization.

Dozens of dirt tracks crisscrossed by "coulisses" (tire imprints) greeted us. "How do you know which path to take?" I wondered, witnessing Ruby's confidence in picking one of them.

"All roads lead to Rome," he said, adding: "All the tracks lead north, eventually meeting by the village. All you have to do is maintain eye contact with the sea, and you can't go wrong."

To the right of the track extended a wide marsh spreading up to the Red Sea, whose water was turquoise blue. To the left there was a yellow desert, studded with small, reddish hills leading to tall mountains with jagged peaks.

A camel traipsing nonchalantly along the narrow sand path we drove on was not impressed at all with the long honk produced by our vehicle at Ruby's behest, and made way slowly. Occasionally, a walking vision was seen on the path, a Bedouin in tatters, wearing a wide sword, with a large comb stuck in his curly mane of hair. They were members of the Edandawa tribe, which makes its living raising camels and selling them in Egypt, after walking seven hundred kilometers (435 miles). Twice a year they move with thousands of camels in a slow march, kicking up clouds of dust that can be seen for kilometers.

Smiling, the amiable Bedouin waved their hands in peace, belying the historical fact that up to the 1940s they were considered the most deadly of Sudan's citizens. Their tradition made it incumbent on every young Edandawa, when he wished to marry, to prove his valor to his bride-to-be and her family. The appropriate proof was at least one scrotum of another tribesman he had killed with his own hands. The first westerners who toured Sudan in the late nineteenth century were still able to see Edandawas returning to base camp from raids on their neighbors, their spears packed with impaled heads and scrota hanging to dry from their camel saddles.

Our Toyota safely negotiated the potholes in the road, marked on the maps as a main axis linking Port Sudan with the Mohammed Gol settlement and the Egyptian border. In Marsa (Lagoon) Darur, a natural bay several kilometers north of the military base, stood huts and cabins built by fishermen and smugglers using the lagoon as their home base. Due to the absence of fresh water, there was no permanent settlement at the spot.

It took us a long time to cover the forty kilometers (twenty-five miles) separating the city and the tourist village.

One need not be a famous economist to realize that without

an established road, there is no way to turn a holiday village into a worthwhile business.

"Not even a phone here," said Ruby. "But the Sudanese are hoping that we, the tourism people from Europe, will be able to do the impossible."

It seems logical that the Italians who built this holiday village chose the Arous lagoon after receiving solemn promises from the governor of the district that work on an asphalt road would start soon.

"Danny and Jonathan got stuck here with the jeep during the rainy season," Ruby said. "The rain runoff comes down from the mountains, and within minutes the entire plain turns into a lake. Luckily for them, they had a load of traditional swords purchased as souvenirs in Kassalah. They beat their swords into shovels and pickaxes and thus were able to extricate the jeep."

We went past a local Bedford truck, heavily laden with passengers and goods. The Bedford driver stood in the middle of the road asking us to stop. "Do you happen to have a strong jack?" he asked in Arabic. One of the passengers translated his words into reasonable English, adding that they had been stuck for a whole day and that the driver's assistant had gone to Port Sudan to get an appropriate jack, and was likely to come back "sometime."

The driver was willing to try to hoist his truck using our Toyota's jack. But we made it clear to him that with all due respect we were not prepared to test the strength of Japanese steel. "No good for truck," we told him. We gave him and the translator cigarettes and moved on.

"That's it, almost there," said Ruby. "I just hope that there is no high tide now and the last section is not flooded, otherwise we will have to make a big detour. One always gets stuck here."

Finally we made it to the edge of the cliff and happily noticed that although the seawater was encroaching on the road, it was very shallow, making it possible for us to cross without difficulty.

Chapter 15

The Toyota climbed with a growl up a not-too-high knoll. From the top, there suddenly emerged very close in front of us something akin to a mirage: a row of some twenty red-roofed bungalows, and a few meters below us, a beautiful turquoise blue lagoon that cut into the land. Besides the bungalows, the hilltop was completely bare, no trees or lawn. It reminded me of old images of the paramilitary Nahal encampment in Ketziot or Beerotaim in the Negev, naturally minus the blue sea in the background. A larger arched structure in the midst of the bungalows was dominant. "This is the kitchen and dining hall," Ruby explained in Hebrew, switching abruptly to English when he saw several white-robed images running out of the building waving their hands enthusiastically. "These are our local employees," Ruby went on. "They've been waiting here, in the middle of nowhere, since the first operation ended about two months ago."

The local people's joy was genuine. Our dust-covered Toyota heralded a much better future.

Since the flight of the Italian entrepreneurs in the mid-1970s, the Government Tourist Corporation had tried to reopen the site, but objective difficulties — distance, lack of communications, absence of fresh water — forced it to give up on the idea. A small team was left behind to watch over and protect the site and the abundant property from the ravages of nature and desert interlopers, in anticipation of some new entrepreneur who might want to breathe a new life into this impossible site.

Now, they believed, a new era of hope was starting in the "Arous Holiday Village." A European company, with connections to the powers that be in Khartoum, had leased the place for a fee of $320,000 for three years. Danny, the company director, his pockets bulging with cash, had toured the area. It was clear to anyone he met that money was no object. They saw the businessman, Danny, buy an expensive jeep and a truck, without even attempting to bargain. He promised to soon send over a team of experts from Europe to spruce up the place in anticipation of thousands of tourists who were already registering at travel agencies across the continent. Anyone listening to his vision was convinced that the influx of tourists would change the economic fortunes not only of the workers at the site but also of hundreds more in the entire region. Any visitor to the site was likely to leave a small tip to the workers, and given the local unemployment rate of 60 percent, a dollar, a French franc or a German mark was a small fortune.

The workers lined up to shake our hands. Here was Hassan, the chief waiter, a smiling forty-year-old, who considered himself worthier than the rest for being Khartoum-born. This snobbishness initially had cost him an unofficial boycott by the local workers. Only Chief Cook Moussa, the head chef, also a Khartoumite, helped break his isolation.

And there was Hashem, who introduced himself as chief cook two, a sous-chef who rushed to the kitchen with Moussa and Hassan to prepare tea and a light meal for us. Ali, the driver, was there too, in the full splendor of the biggest mane of curly hair I had ever seen; and Hashem Issa, the guard, who didn't stop smiling with a wide-eyed stare. Ali, the driver, gestured to us behind Hashem's back that he was "slightly deranged." There were several other men as well, charged with other duties.

The Arous Holiday Village was stunningly beautiful. Anyone who has been to Sharm-el-Sheikh, and is familiar with the concrete monsters constructed by Israeli entrepreneurs along the Naama Bay seafront, could not help admiring the work of the Italian architect who managed to blend the structures at Arous into the natural landscape to the point of oblivion.

The dining hall, in front of a large kitchen, was the center of activity. It exuded a holiday atmosphere. It had no doors or windows but rather arches, which brought in the myriad hues of the Red Sea, tinted by the many coral reefs. Simple straw awnings over the openings were enough to protect the structure from sand-storms or an unexpected rain shower. The floor was paved with red terra-cotta tiles, and standing there were simple, wide wooden tables and matching chairs upholstered in blue. In the center was a small reception counter, and alongside it a small bar, adorned with a photo of Nimeiri, somewhat faded due to salt and moisture. The kitchen was well equipped, but the electrical appliances did not work. The level of filth would have shocked any average sanitation inspector. But we were hungry and ate the fried fish that Hassan brought us and enjoyed the tea chaser.

Chapter 16

After eating, we went looking around the village. To the left and right of the dining hall stood smaller structures. Each structure held two small bedrooms with wooden floors, a queen-sized bed, a cabinet and a disabled air conditioner, coveted both by birds and giant lizards as a habitat.

Each room had a shower, sink and a European toilet. The rooms were simple but comfortable, almost Hilton quality considering that they were located in the middle of the desert. The two best maintained rooms were kept by Hassan for us, the European managers. I put my bag in the room that was to be my home for the next three months. Then, Ruby and I continued our tour of the village.

In the northern part of the village stood a number of storage rooms with equipment harking back to the Italian era, starting with old buoys, spear guns for underwater fishing, mostly with torn rubber springs, and old and dusty tarpaulins. A small crater held the generator house. "The Italians poured millions of lira into development," I was thinking to myself as we examined the generators. They had spared neither effort nor money, and brought in the very best of everything. The two German-made Magirus Deutz generators were so powerful that they could light up half of Port Sudan.

Apparently, the Italians did believe that a road was going to be constructed to the area, or else one fails to understand why they made such a huge investment in constructing a tourist site of this size in a place that has no water, electricity or telephone infrastructure. To keep the generators going, a tanker truck needed to go at least twice a week to Port Sudan, an almost impossible mission considering the condition of the southbound dirt track and the empty gasoline tanks in Port Sudan.

"*Shaghal*, it's working," Ali, the driver who also doubled as a generator mechanic, exclaimed proudly. He removed the battery from our Toyota and hooked it up to one of the generators. Following this, he poured two drops of machine oil into a black opening and pressed a button. One of the generators did start clanking and creaking, belching a cloud of thick blue smoke, which disappeared as soon as the clanking noise became steady.

"You see, it is working," Ali said, affectionately patting the body of the giant metal monster. But even excellent German-made generators can't overcome years of neglect and no maintenance. Within a few minutes the generator began choking and making strange noises. The gauge showed that electrical power was being produced, but since there is no bulb in existence that can feed off the fluctuating current that was being produced by the generator, Ali threw his hands up in the air, as if to say, "What can I do, that's what there is." He pressed a button marked *AUS*, meaning "off" in German. The generator died.

At the foot of the hill, at the southern edge of the village, on the bank of the lagoon itself, stood a small cabin which served for storing equipment for the boats. Some outboard motors of the Mercury 40 series, a green stripe running around them, stood on improvised stands. "We received them directly from the Israel Navy ship *Bat Galim*," Ruby whispered. "The green stripe conceals the military markings, in Hebrew of course, and serial numbers issued by the Israeli navy." Ruby's explanation provided me with a final proof that our activity in Sudan was governed by totally different rules than those I had known in the past. I also understood now that the superficial briefing we received before heading out from Khartoum, which led to our arrest in Kheir, was no exception for this unit. In our operation, sometimes the basic, "by the book" rules of covert operation were not applied. A long series of minor glitches and several real failures that were to crop up later retroactively vindicated this theory.

On the waterline stood several antiquated fiberglass flat bottom boats, a legacy from the Italian era in the village.

"Lousy boats — we used them in the first operation," Ruby whispered. "They're no good. Unstable and water permeable. You can imagine how the Ethiopian Jews, who had never seen the sea, panicked when they were put into these walnut shells. We almost had a disaster. From now on, we only use Zodiacs, inflatable rubber dinghies."

Next door was the diving equipment depot, a housing unit converted to its current use, which held a long row of shiny compressed air tanks, a portable compressor to refill them, a cabinet stuffed with diving suits, masks, flippers, knives and everything needed for the smooth operation of an efficient diving club. Ruby scanned the equipment, which had set the Israeli taxpayer back tens of thousands of dollars, with a loving gaze. It provided a plausible enough cover story, enabling us to work freely in Sudan in order to rescue Jewish refugees.

In this room we also set up our camouflaged communication gear to help us maintain daily contact with headquarters. It needed an aerial to ensure decent quality transmissions. Aware that the best cover story is the closest to reality, we placed a completely innocuous domestic radio set on one of the shelves, took a thin electrical wire and extended it to the nearby structure and hooked it up to the radio. "We put the aerial in to be able to tune in to the BBC properly," we told Hassan and Ali, who accepted the explanation unquestioningly. In order to make sure local workers wouldn't peek inside the room, we set up a small wardrobe for the divers, spread heavy curtains on the windows, and labeled the "cloakroom" out of bounds.

"What's this heap of metal?" I asked Ruby on seeing a pile of pipes and containers placed behind the shack. "This is a sophisticated water desalination system which was never unpacked because no one even bothered to try to put it together," he explained.

Hassan provided further details. It turned out that this equipment had been worth millions of dollars — a perfect example of a botched and misguided foreign aid program.

"The builders wanted to set up a small seawater desalination system," he said. "One day a convoy of trucks showed up carrying all these pipes and crates. We were told that this was a Danish-made system donated by Kuwait to Sudan to prop up its flagging economy. The Italian engineer who checked it said that he wanted a small, compact system, and that the Kuwaitis were surely out of their minds, since this system is capable of providing drinking water to an entire city, as well as enough water to irrigate several large agricultural farms. Expected running costs were so high and required so much fuel that the Italians didn't bother unpacking."

Armed with a long stick, for fear of waking up sleeping snakes, I began rummaging through the pile of metal pipes and heavy crates. Six or seven years of exposure to the scorching desert sun had caused the original blue paint to fade and peel off. Rubber parts had cracked. In some places there were signs of unauthorized unpacking by local thieves, who must have cannibalized parts suitable for improvised uses. Each crate was tagged "Made in Denmark."

"Why Denmark?" I was thinking to myself. The Danes may suffer from lack of sunshine, but why dabble in seawater desalination? As a news reporter I once aired a story about water desalination projects in Israel using the Alexander Zarhin method. And based on my broad knowledge, I ventured a speculative thought: "If this isn't an Israeli-made contraption, I'm king of Prussia."

I opened more crates, scratching the grime off tiny metal plates, which also bore out that it was Danish-made equipment. Finally, however, on a remote corner of a large metal container, I found what I had been looking for: a small Hebrew inscription, probably that of one of the subcontractors, which had escaped the scrutiny of those who were supposed to supervise the whole thing. This made me emerge from the bowels of the heap of equipment with a broad smile, knowing that Israel did make a small profit from the oil crisis of the mid-1970s.

The Kuwaitis, dizzy with an endless flow of dollars resulting from the sharp hike in oil prices, bought a desalination facility in Denmark without checking who the manufacturer was and made a gift of it to Sudan. The fact that this facility had not produced even one cubic centimeter of desalinated seawater did not bother anyone. The main thing is that dollars were transferred from one bank account to another and that everyone, including the Israeli manufacturer, was happy.

Chapter 17

Ruby and I began work almost immediately. We were supposed to ready the village for visitors at short notice, or at least pretend that we were working toward this end. The first pressing problem was fresh water supply shortage. A deep cistern in the center of the village served as our water reservoir. An electrical pump took the precious fluid to a small tower, and pipelines built by the Italians were supposed to take it to the rooms. A simple matter, on the face of it, but in practice there were many setbacks.

Large sections of the system were plugged with sand, and the northern bungalows got no water at all. The same went for the tank atop the tower because the generator was unable to function longer than a few minutes at a time. A Bedouin delivering buckets of water to the rooms would be a perfect subject for an exotic photograph, but that wasn't a long-term solution.

The malfunctioning generator went beyond the water problem — no power means no refrigerators or air conditioners. During the months of January and February one can manage without air conditioners, but from March to December the site turns into a hot, moist furnace.

As our inspection wore on, the checklist of things requiring thorough treatment became longer. Every new item on the list made it clear to us that the idea of setting up a holiday village to serve as a cover for an operation to rescue Ethiopian Jews from Sudan was bound to cost the Israeli taxpayer a lot of money over the next three years.

This was duly reported to headquarters. The following day, apparently after deep consideration, they came back with an answer which wasn't to our liking at all: "In the meantime, don't run too many expenses. Continue to make lists and noise, but explain that you are waiting for the arrival of the general manager who, God willing, should arrive this month."

Having deciphered the kind answer, Ruby and I turned into real Bedouin, taking it easy all the time. And the following is a correct representation of what we did for the next two weeks.

The absence of electricity dictated the schedule of our work.

The day started with a good breakfast in the dining hall, which overlooked the lagoon, and included tea or coffee, juice from a can probably past expiry date, and fresh rolls baked by Hashem and Hassan. After breakfast, we ran a brief inspection tour, mostly to show the flag, and later were free to take care of food supplies, namely fishing.

Hashem Issa, the guard, took care to fill up the red fuel tanks for the Mercury motors in the boat equipment depot. A fully equipped Zodiac was already waiting for us on the water's edge. Ruby took full diving gear. I had to make do with a snorkel only, since my brief diving career had been aborted due to an accident three years earlier, not connected to underwater activity. "May I dive again?" I asked the doctor who signed my release papers from the hospital. "Go ahead," he replied, "if you really want to commit suicide, but I believe you'd be better off purchasing a handgun — it would be quicker and cheaper."

And that was why I had to observe one of the world's most fascinating diving sites from the surface, feeling much like the subject of the Arabic proverb "like a deaf person at a wedding procession (traditionally a noisy affair, including drums and cymbals)."

The exit from the Arous lagoon to the sea was through a narrow passage flanked on each side by coral reefs. The area is full of such reefs. True, they are marked on maps, but anyone trusting the maps alone will soon enough find himself stuck on one, which according to the records should have been a few hundred meters farther ahead. Even our Zodiac couldn't cross the reefs, which stretched across the horizon, without breaking the propeller blades, even though it had a draft of a few centimeters only.

"Despite all the preparatory work and advance reconnaissance,

during the first operation all the boats hit reefs, motors got bent
— don't ask what a mess that was," described Ruby.

After a few minutes' drive we reached one of the reefs and cast
anchor. Ruby checked his equipment carefully yet again, constantly
repeating his pet statement: "Accidents do not happen, they are
caused. Routine is a diver's worst enemy." Finally Ruby asked, mimicking a chief steward at a high-priced French restaurant: "Will
monsieur have the grouper or a baby shark?" Then, waving his
hand, he disappeared into the turquoise blue water, leaving a trail
of bubbles on the surface.

During one of these diving episodes, I witnessed an unplanned
encounter with a shark. I watched it from my safe vantage point
atop the reef. The shark, about three meters long, coveted the fat
fish that Ruby had caught and hung from a metal wire wrapped
around his waist. The veteran diver, who had run into a lot of sharks
in his career, wasn't intimidated by the gray predator and quickly
clung to the reef. He knew that because of the shape of its mouth,
located at the bottom of the head, the shark is unable to snap at
anyone clinging to a wall or a coral rise.

"He was quite nice," Ruby said, reconstructing the incident
some time later. "I returned his kindness and gave him a fish. But
the bastard decided that if he got one finger there was no reason for
him not to take the entire hand. He started whirling around me. I
gave him yet another fish, but this was not enough to satisfy him.
He came closer and even started rubbing against me."

Observed from above, it didn't look like a happy occasion at
all. The shark's circles drew closer. And then I saw the last thing I
expected to happen: Ruby's hand shot forward and punched the
shark directly in the nose. The great predator responded by taking
flight into deep water. It wasn't prepared for the possibility that a
strange black-finned creature with two air tanks on its back, continuously releasing bubbles like a frightened whale, would punch
him, the king of marine predators.

Back in the Zodiac, Ruby smoked a cigarette and gently mas-
saged an injury to a knuckle, the result of the deliberate blow to

the rough skin on the shark's snout. He explained: "I decided that my kindness had run out. It got two fish already but was still after the dinner of Hassan, Moussa and the rest of our loyal workers. So, when he came closer yet again, I smacked him right in the nose."

"It's nice that this ended the way it did," I answered, still pondering the bizarre scene I had just witnessed. "What epitaph would we inscribe on your headstone at Kiryat Shaul Military Cemetery in Tel Aviv? 'Devoured in the line of duty?'"

"A whale of a life," said Ruby, stretching along the side of the Zodiac. "Things aren't too bad as they are."

Minutes later, we returned to our makeshift dock, where Hassan and Hashem were waiting for us to expedite the fishes' way into the pan.

While the local crew was busy preparing the fish and other food, Ruby plunged into his second-favorite pastime (after diving): improving his tan. Wearing a minimal swimsuit, lying on a colorful deckchair, with matches separating his fingers "so the sun can reach everywhere" and an earphone stuck in his ear to pick up Israel Radio's second channel broadcasts, he didn't look at all like a secret agent of the State of Israel in the midst of covert activity.

"It's crazy, it's up again," he communicated the latest Tel Aviv stock market report to me. In the winter of 1982, trading was producing a continuous string of higher quotes. And thus, on the Red Sea shore, about three thousand kilometers (over eighteen hundred miles) south of the Stock Exchange building in Tel Aviv, Ruby was rattling off names of stocks such as IDB, where he invested the money he received in compensation for the house he was forced to abandon in Nueba during the Israeli pullback from Sinai.

In the diving gear depot I found a pair of water skis and decided that this was the opportunity to improve my water skiing, which was entirely instinctual and hardly elegant.

Ruby hastened to make it clear to me that since he was in his total Bedouin period, he had no intention of disrupting the atmosphere of tranquility by whirling around the lagoon in a noisy Zodiac trailing a rope at the end of which I proposed to polish my skiing style. Ruby's impenetrable calm prompted me to promote Hashem the guard to his new role.

After nearly an hour of hand movements and pantomime à la Marcel Marceau — I didn't want anyone in the village to know that I had full command of Arabic — I gave Hashem a basic course in operating a Zodiac with a powerful Mercury outboard motor. Together we developed our own sign language, when he should accelerate, what he should do to keep the boat running at the edge of the lagoon and avoid hitting the reefs, as well as some precautionary measures.

The hours I spent with Hashem in the lagoon produced an endless series of incidents. We enjoyed every minute and so, I believe, did the offspring of the pink pelicans that wandered at the water's edge watching us. Every time we went roaring into their lagoon, their numbers would increase.

At the start, Hashem had trouble coordinating his weight with the boat's movement. This was a problem when he insisted on accelerating while standing up on the boat's wooden floor. I explained to him that he had better sit on the rubber side panel, but he wouldn't give in. Whenever I signaled to him to give full throttle, he would lose his balance and fall heavily into the water as the boat accelerated. In anticipation of such cases, the throttle was equipped with a special spring, which, in the absence of a gripping hand, would slow the motor down to a minimum and shunt the wheel sideways. In our case, this would send the boat on slow rotations, and Hashem, who swam behind it in Sudanese "freestyle," had no trouble latching onto it. Anyhow, the first few times this happened, I almost died from swallowing water while laughing hysterically.

One day, Hashem, who apparently already considered himself an expert at running Zodiacs, averted his eyes from the planned course in front of him. I waved to him frenetically to signal that he should watch it as we were getting too close to the edge of the lagoon, but Hashem, mistaking my signal for a friendly gesture, acknowledged with a similar wave of the hand, which was sus-

pended within seconds as the Zodiac raced full speed forward
onto the reef. Hashem flew forward, in what a sportscaster would
call a double flic-flac. His momentum was slowed however by an
unplanned encounter with the boat's rubber bow, which probably
saved his head from the unpleasant, or even fatal, experience of
being smeared on a particularly sharp edge of the reef. The massive
bang he took didn't wipe the broad smile off his face. "Great. It was
great," he told me in Arabic, and I confirmed his observation with
a nod of the head.

The damage to the motor was negligible, and so our daily practice went on, but this time Hashem took care to keep his eyes on
our course.

Chapter 18

At night we would spend hours sitting in deckchairs and gazing at the stars. Only those who have experienced a night in the desert, far from any populated places, will know what I am talking about. The sky, from horizon to horizon, is densely crowded with myriad spots of light. A halo to the east marked the location of the Saudi Arabian port city of Jeddah, about a hundred kilometers (sixty miles) away. Occasionally, an aircraft would pass between the stars high in the sky, leaving behind a muffled echo.

Many times during my stay in Sudan, I spent the night in the desert, far from populated places. Sitting in the midst of this amazing silence, only occasionally disturbed by the cry of an animal, is a rare experience for most westerners. Lying on your back in the soft sand and gazing at the skies closing in from every direction like a giant roof makes it clear why Moses, Elijah, Jeremiah, Jesus, Mohammed and many others fled to the desert and came back with stories about marvelous revelations and encounters with the holy spirit in all its manifestations.

One evening we thought we were headed for an encounter of the third kind with the Creator. We were sitting in deckchairs, observing the reflection of the moon in the still water of the Red Sea, when the singing of Matti Caspi, a well-known Israeli entertainer, reached our ears. I no longer remember what song it was, but then sitting in a godforsaken spot in Sudan, thousands of kilometers from Israel, Ruby and I, both confirmed atheists, were not entirely convinced that it was Caspi's voice and not that of an angel in God's celestial choir.

We got up and started marching in the direction of the voice. The voice was blaring from the village dining hall. As we drew near, we saw our local crew around a bonfire, drinking araq in quantities that could fell any European, swaying to a Matti Caspi song coming off a large transistor radio placed on the ground.

"*Tfadalu*, welcome," said Hassan, inviting us with a broad sweep of the hand to join the circle of celebrants. We gladly did.

"Nice music — what is it?" we curiously asked our hosts.

"I have no idea," Ali answered in Arabic, his eyes glazed with alcoholic stupor and tobacco chewing. "*Yunani*," Hassan, the man of the world from Khartoum, hastened to translate: "Greek, Greek music."

I looked at the radio set. The dial stood at the far end of the scale. The song ended that second, and the announcer in the Channel Three studio in Jerusalem started describing the shimmering rain-washed roofs she saw on her way to work, voicing her longing for a European winter accompanied by white snowflakes, and put on a record by Yves Montand with a chanson about dead leaves and a sense of autumn at heart.

"*Yunani*," Ali kept repeating the word as though reciting a mantra. "It's the very best there is," he said in Arabic.

After a week's stay at the village, Ali and I drove to Port Sudan to shop for groceries at the "haphazard selection" store owned by our Indian friend, in a brand new International truck left by Danny. Ali was a consummate driver; he knew how to hit a pothole and get out of it. It can be said that the trip was very pleasant. Ali also provided entertainment, singing along at the top of his voice accompanying local music blaring from a cassette in the truck.

It was then that our water problem was partially resolved. It turned out that just outside our village there were a number of springs with outstanding water quality, and that they belonged to the local power company. I used our visit to meet one of its directors. In return for a not-too-fat wad of Sudanese pounds, and an open invitation to him and his family members to enjoy the facilities at our holiday village, he penned a formal document which allowed an Arous Holiday Village tanker truck, a rickety vehicle with a five-thousand-liter capacity, to frequent the site "as needed."

The remaining problem now was fuel for the generators. We drove up to the Shell refinery. Dozens of tanker trucks were already there awaiting their turn to enter the facility. In such cases, you appreciate how easy it is to act colonial. At the sight of a European — me — in the cabin, the gatekeeper quickly opened the metal gate without questions or need to present papers.

In one of the offices sat the deputy manager of the installation, an amiable, smiling Briton, under a brand new Japanese-made air conditioner, his eyes slightly glazed perhaps on account of the Sudanese sun, or loneliness. Queen Elizabeth II's subjects in Sudan were happy to talk with anyone who tried to strike up a conversation with them. This stood in sharp contrast to the reserved image of the British. He quickly offered me a glass of whiskey and fired off a string of questions. After the second glass, his questions started getting somewhat too specific, so I switched to shorter answers, still supplied in a pleasant manner.

On the subject of fuel, I was treated to another lesson in Africanology. "I have no fuel problem. You can get as much as you want, as long as you are willing to pay me a realistic price. The government wants to make a profit on our backs, because the tax on fuel is one of the few sources of income it has. But at the price they set for me, I lose money. So, I make it known that the tanks are empty. But for a pal like you, I'll always manage to scrape together a few hundred liters."

He too gave me a document which could have solved the gasoline and heating fuel issue for the Arous Holiday Village for a number of years to come.

Happy and content, I returned to the village, prepared and ready to enjoy a life of leisure that almost made me forget why we had come to Sudan — extricating Jewish refugees whose lives were in peril.

Chapter 19

It was quiet in the wadi. Far too quiet. And pitch black. I had four layers of clothes on, including a parka, but this was not enough to keep the desert cold out of our bones on this late January night.

I was trembling slightly, because of the cold and for fear of the unknown.

"Where the hell are they?" Ruby asked softly. "They" were Ethiopian Jews from Tawawa, the largest refugee camp in the region.

The wind drifting in from Tawawa filled the air with the scents typical of Africa: a blend of smoke and a non-specific odor of a wheat and barley dish cooking on hundreds of small bonfires lighting up the night sky.

The small wadi next to Gedaref was the meeting place where Danny had arranged to take in the Jews and put them on our trucks. There were a number of Israelis there, all with borrowed identities. Marcel was Danny's number two.

Shlomo Pomeranz, I recalled, was the tall Israeli who gave Ruby and me the Toyota pickup truck in the Hilton Hotel parking lot. Despite the total compartmentalization of his activity in Khartoum — arranging for Jews to leave semi-legally with the aid of an international refugee assistance organization — headquarters may have had their own considerations in arranging for us to meet, or else someone in Sudanese top echelons was sitting on a Swiss bank dollar account opened for him in return for turning a blind eye on our activities.

Dr. Pomeranz had full command of English at mother-tongue level, and spoke with a North-American accent. He appeared to enjoy taking motors apart and putting them back together again. His hands were always black with machine oil.

"Tell me, is it really a Jewish Agency operation?" The surprising question came from Shmulik in the middle of the highly charged operation, steeped in tension and apprehension.

Shmulik was a perfect example of what Danny's "Foreign Legion" was all about: a handsome man, well built, black haired, about thirty-five years old, born for the sea, who had uncanny knowledge of the Red Sea fish population. He was a consummate diving instructor and a master of improvisation. He was recruited in the fall of 1981 by Danny for the first marine operation, an adventure that nearly cost him his marriage. His wife was about to give birth at the time, and he managed to come up with a lame explanation about his work for the "Agency." His command of foreign languages extended to saying "*Yasu*" in Greek and speaking Pinglish (Palestinian English), but none of this prevented this brave and amiable man from functioning in an outstanding manner.

When Danny asked him in January 1982 to repeat the operation, he promptly agreed and that was the reason for our sitting together in the open truck cabin, exposed to winds and freezing cold.

After getting over Shmulik's question, I couldn't help smiling. A perfectly normal man gets up one morning, leaves his business and his family and equipped with a fake passport travels to an Arab country to save Jews, risking his life, all without even knowing who he is working for.

I remained silent. Operationally, in case of a problem or capture, he had better believe that we were "Agency" employees. But I decided that if the mission went well, I would tell him who was really behind this entire operation.

The hackneyed phrase "one could cut the tension with a knife," so much liked by detective novel writers, fit the situation to a tee. Shmulik, who was a skilled knifeman, excelling in the quick draw and well-aimed throw to a distance of a few meters, spent his time cleaning the knife with measured motions, apparently attempting to overcome the tension.

"Try to explain to a nosy cop what you, a European white man, are doing in the middle of the night in this godforsaken spot, with two run-down trucks, carrying jerry cans of water and oil drums, a few kilometers away from the Ethiopian border," Dr. Pomeranz said in a soft voice.

"What's the problem?" I said, trying to sound funny. "We'll give him our cover story, that we're looking for the Swedish female volunteers at the Red Cross hospital in Kassala, with whom we have arranged to spend the night."

"Very funny," said Marcel. "Believe me, this operation has more holes in it than Swiss cheese."

Going out for a date with the shapely female volunteers of the Swedish hospital in Kassala was the cover story we concocted for the benefit of the village workers, who wondered where we were disappearing to, just when the refurbishment and preparations for the reopening of the facility moved into high gear. To do justice to Hassan, Ali and their colleagues, they figured out quickly enough that the Europeans who settled in the village were a bunch of weirdos or crazies. Under the circumstances, a cover story that included shapely Swedish women waiting for us on the other side of the desert appeared plausible to them.

Who knows how our dedicated workers explained our taking dozens of plastic jerry cans full of drinking water with us. Perhaps they thought that nutcases like us take care to bathe in the middle of the desert before a hot session with Swedish bombshells. No one knows. As time wore on, our "sex sorties" became too frequent to be explained by excessive hormonal activity, and they began suspecting that things weren't "kosher." But as long as their higher-than-average salaries were paid regularly, and the food they were served was reasonable, they chose to keep their mouths shut.

To be honest, I didn't believe that we would be able to carry out our plans. The condition of our four vehicles — which wouldn't have passed the road worthiness tests in Israel, even with a bribe to the licensing mechanic — aptly attested to the poor preparations. Danny drove one Toyota pickup truck, and Marcel the other Toyota pickup that had given us so much trouble on the way to the village. Ruby, Shmulik, Dr. Pomeranz and I were responsible for two run-down trucks, one an American-made International, and the other a yellow Japanese truck made by Hino, a company that in the 1960s supplied auto parts to a small assembly plant in Haifa which produced two cars: "Contessa 900" and "Contessa 1300." The company later bowed to the Arab boycott, abandoned the small Israeli market and did well exporting trucks and buses to Arab countries, Sudan included.

The trucks were modified to the Sudanese standard: two large tires in the rear and a high cargo box with reinforced sides. The driver's cabin had been removed entirely, save the front windscreen. In its place, a squarish wood and metal structure was built, which allowed four to six people to be seated comfortably, albeit without doors or windows, the absence of which we experienced when we raced to Gedaref at night, cursing the freezing wind that lashed at us mercilessly. Even smoking was impossible in this open cabin. We discovered this when a flying spark set the seat of the Hino truck on fire — a result of my attempt to smoke while driving. The spark lodged itself in the seat's coarse cotton upholstery, ate its way deeper into the raw cotton balls that made up the filling material of the seat, and suddenly, due to a fresh gust of wind that fanned it, set my rear end and the seat on fire.

I stopped the vehicle in horror and put out the fire. Trembling with cold, I wrapped a scarf around my head, Sudanese style, and in utter despair started talking in rhymes. "On the way to Kassala, I'm feeling like a frozen fish fillet, Out of the sea of old Norway, God only knows how it will end one day." This was what I told Danny when he came up to our truck to find out what was happening.

Our morale was low. The fire incident was made all the more terrifying by the fact that our clothes were soggy with fuel oil splashed during our improvised refueling attempts. Seeing that proper gas stations existed only in the big towns, five hundred kilometers (about three hundred miles) away from Gedaref, refueling was done with the aid of a rubber hose, one end stuck inside a drum of fuel, and the other stuck into the gas tank. It worked only after the air was sucked out of the hose, a manipulation that often sent a jet of fuel oil into our mouths and splashed our clothes.

We were hungry. We had left the village loaded down with bags of biscuits and rusks (hard bread crisps), and crates of fruit that bore only a remote resemblance to any known fruit species.

We were also tired. We had been on the road for two days waiting for confirmation from headquarters to go ahead. But as if deliberately, communications with headquarters and the other bodies involved in the mission were touch and go. "It's all because of sun spots," someone volunteered an explanation. "It's a very bad year for wireless communication." No one had the strength to try to disprove this theory.

Chapter 20

On the third day, Danny decided that it was impossible to go on. "I don't know what happened to Uri, our contact in Khartoum. Apparently there are problems with the navy. Until things are sorted out, we'll try to get ourselves a better setup," he said. "We're going to the government guesthouse in Gedaref."

We left the highway and entered Gedaref. To the left and to the right, almost up to the horizon, the area was filled with thousands of little shacks, made of straw, cardboard crates, boards and sheets of tin, which were actually encampments of hundreds of thousands of miserable refugees from neighboring countries. They included Jews who were to become Israeli citizens within forty-eight hours, but did not yet know it. We who were supposed to help them realize their dream of "Return to Zion" didn't believe at that moment that this operation would end successfully.

Gedaref itself was made up of small homes, two stories at the most. Tiny shops dotted its dusty streets. They had a poor selection of merchandise, mostly cans of food stolen from food aid shipments. The entire town of some hundred thousand souls, refugees excluded, had no functioning gas station, decent restaurant or reasonable hotel — only poverty, deprivation, dust, flies and a massive military and police presence.

The government guesthouse lay in the midst of a military camp. The sleepy sentry jumped with concern at the sight of the small convoy that pulled up with squealing brakes. He looked with amazement at the two pickup trucks and the other two larger trucks and their occupants, white men with dust-covered faces.

"We are employees of the Tourism Ministry," Danny said nonchalantly, pulling out an official document, adorned with signatures in different hues. The most weighty one was that of a senior personality, a high-ranking army officer, who knew as much about tourism as we did and had done nothing for promoting the tourist industry in his country. But, he was ready to do anything for Danny, who had visited his office one day, put $320,000 on his desk and rented the abandoned Arous Holiday Village for three years. I have no conclusive proof, but part of the lease fees may have ended up in the colonel's private bank account. Since this is the way business is conducted in Sudan, I don't think I'm too far off the mark. After such a lucrative deal, the colonel was sure to have equipped Danny with every possible reference.

The manager of the guesthouse reached the gate at a light trot. He examined the papers, saluted and told the sentry to open the gate.

The government guesthouse in Gedaref was nothing but a small camp of tin shacks, on the verge of total ruin, which were inherited from the British army. The accommodations had no doors, no windows, a dripping water faucet in every room and iron frame beds with moldy mattresses, but at least they had a roof and walls. It was also possible to buy hot tea for a few pennies.

Exhausted, we got out of the vehicles. Ahead of us, relaxing in a tattered deckchair, was a well-groomed European man, about forty-five years old, dressed in a nice safari suit. He looked at us closely. To a chance observer he looked like a colonial official who had failed to leave town in 1956, when the Union Jack was folded in a somber ceremony. He greeted us with a perfect British accent while blowing a huge cloud of smoke from his pipe.

Danny, Marcel and I, who had met the person who greeted us under other circumstances, almost burst out laughing, managing to remain poker-faced with great difficulty. We responded cordially to his words. Dr. Pomeranz decided to ignore the man, who was none other than Uri, our man in Khartoum. Because of total compartmentalization, we were prohibited from showing publicly that we knew him.

Uri was responsible for keeping contact with the Jews in the camps, with the help of a network of activists, handpicked from amongst the Ethiopian Jews. I have no words to describe the courage of those young men who at great personal risk worked in refugee camps crawling with secret police agents and innumerable informers. Their main task was locating Jews among the refugees and handing them assistance money from the Mossad, usually passed through Uri. The amounts were very modest, so as not to arouse suspicion among the other refugees — who were not aware of the Jews in their midst — but enough to keep them from starving. These activists, whom we called "Committee men" (they had formed a group they dubbed "the Committee"), were also responsible for contact with the families and getting them ready for departure.

Thus Uri was the key to our operation. We had tried to reach him but without success. In our despair, we had decided to take time out and go to the guesthouse instead. But fate intervened and here he was sitting without a care in the world on the balcony, in the company of Sudanese officers and local government officials, as if this were a prearranged meeting place. It was yet another indication that someone above very much wanted our mission to succeed.

We quickly got ourselves together in the room assigned to us by the manager, and each took a quick shower, which despite the thin trickle of water left us feeling a lot better. Danny and Uri managed a secret powwow for a few minutes to coordinate the next moves. The only problem that remained now was reporting to headquarters.

"It's best to call from the outhouse," I told Danny. We took the camouflaged radio and slipped into the remote structure that served as a most basic military-style toilet. It consisted of small booths with big pits. The stench was horrible, and only our trust in the vaccinations administered in the public clinics at home steeled us to the thought that the giant flies zooming through the air would land on us seconds after making a sweep through the stinking trenches.

But the outhouse had a marked advantage, at least from the

wireless communication point of view. There was enough room to extend the antenna and the narrow windows enabled those inside — in this case Danny and I — to notice anyone approaching.

We pulled out the instrument with record alacrity, attached the aerial, and with a press of a button released a detailed, coded report broadcast beginning with these words: "This is a direct broadcast from the government guesthouse latrine in Gedaref." It was well received in Tel Aviv.

That night we slept like logs. In the morning, after drinking the traditional glass of tea, we took leave of all the people at the site, including Uri, who was already sitting in his deckchair on the balcony, pulling on his pipe. The manager's smile was particularly wide, for a reason: he received dozens of Sudanese pounds — a small fortune — for lodging us, which promptly ended up in his own pocket.

Chapter 21

A few hours remained before the operation was to start. We spent the day in a small wadi not far from Gedaref. True, we were feeling better, but we still thought that the best title for this operation was "A catastrophe waiting for a time and place to happen." Even Danny's unbridled enthusiasm failed to work. The operational plan was simple but fraught with risks. Our vehicles were in terrible shape, the dirty fuel plugged the carburetors and we didn't have enough spare tires in case flats occurred.

"Everything'll be fine," Danny kept saying while scratching his head through frizzled hair. "Believe me. Everything'll be alright."

I personally hate the "Everything'll be fine" style. Not that I'm the epitome of planning, but perhaps because of my Yekke (German-Jewish) background, I never counted on this method that has made the people of Israel masters of improvisation, at least in operational matters.

An English historian was asked once why the British army awards so few medals to its soldiers, compared with the Red Army for instance, whose soldiers return home with decorations covering their chests. "A medal or a citation is usually an expression of failure or chaos that should not have happened had everything been properly planned from the outset," was his curt answer.

But truth be told, throughout Sudan I found out time and again that an operational plan based on "Everything'll be fine" can work after all.

In any case, these were Danny's parting words as he left a short time after sunset for the refugee camps ringing Gedaref. Ferede was already there locating his men and waiting for word from Danny about the time and place of the pickup.

Anyone who expects a description of a sophisticated operation, brimming with technical stunts, is in for disappointment. The plan was simplicity itself. Danny, Uri and Ferede were supposed to meet under cover of darkness with the Committee men and give them the sign to act. For fear of deliberate leaks or exposure due to nosy neighbors, the Jews were not given advance warning. They had been on permanent standby to leave their shacks secretly, leaving the fire burning in the ovens and taking very few possessions wrapped in a blanket or a kerchief. And thus, family after family, the Jews slipped clandestinely out of the camps and guided by Committee men, walked in the dark to the pickup point.

We were waiting in the dark, the side panels of our trucks lowered and ready to take in the arrivals. Several hundred meters away there was a faint movement of trucks and pickup trucks, with an occasional flicker of blue light from a passing police patrol car.

We were concerned about being informed on or that successful police surveillance would detect the refugees leaving the camps surreptitiously. We imagined how all of a sudden, dozens of uniformed men, armed with Kalashnikov assault rifles, would try to storm us, shrieking wildly. In such a case, we were supposed to flee, run for our lives. Unlike actors in action films, we carried no weapons: we weren't keen to go to jail for many years because of a needless gun battle with local law enforcement representatives, or to cause casualties to either side.

In the meantime, nothing happened. We continued to hear familiar night sounds: the rumble of a heavy truck on the road, the shriek of a night bird, the rustle of a frightened animal that suddenly found its hunting path blocked by a large body of metal. A pair of headlights left the road heading our way. A minute later the lights went out, but then we were able to recognize the sound of Danny's Toyota, navigating solely by moonlight.

Marcel peeked at his watch. "That's it. The 'brothers' are on their way and are due here any minute now."

Our trembling, so far the result of the cold, was intensifying because of the tension and excitement.

"All's well," announced Danny. "The meeting with the

Committee men went like clockwork. They promised to arrange the exodus of the Jews from the camps quietly."

We checked our vehicles once again. The nicotine addicts among us lit up another cigarette before the "action."

A sharp whistle cut the silence. Suddenly, like a picture out of a ghost horror film, hundreds of images stood up and started sliding into the wadi. It turned out that while we were waiting, hundreds of Jews had arrived, and guided by Committee men, gathered in amazing silence at the wadi's edge close by. There were old people, women, children and babies, and we didn't hear them at all. We only noticed them as they rose to the whistle to climb onto the vehicles.

Years later, in a Tel Aviv pub, I met a senior army officer who took part in securing a subsequent operation. "I'll have you know, Gadi, that the Ethiopians are born infantrymen," he said enthusiastically. "What soldiership, what limberness, what stamina! There are ten Ethiopian soldiers in my battalion and I would love to have more. When they close in on a target at night, I can't see or hear them, as long as they don't smile, because their white teeth give them away."

I knew exactly what he was talking about.

The boarding was over within minutes. Each truck, by our estimate, had almost a hundred Jews, packed like sardines. The closed box of the Toyota held another twenty. The heavy straw matting we had attached to the sides of the truck hid everything inside from view.

The Committee men got on the trucks to brief the passengers. They shushed them and quickly listed a number of precautionary measures. "You are now going on a trip that will take long hours. The police are after you, and therefore you must not stick arms or heads out of the truck. Mothers must take care to calm crying children. Even if the truck stops, silence must be maintained, because it may have stopped because of a police roadblock. Getting off the vehicle will be strictly on orders from Danny or his men. If the police catch you, say you are refugees from Ethiopia, who were promised work on a big farm in the Port Sudan area. Even if they keep pressing, don't change your story, and under no condition are you to let on that you are Jews."

The activists got off the vehicles and rounded up the "brothers" who couldn't fit into the trucks despite all the compression efforts, to take them back to the refugee camp. Before saying goodbye, the activists came up to shake our hands. "*Shalom*," one said in Hebrew. "See you in Jerusalem."

Within seconds they disappeared into the darkness.

Chapter 22

We started the vehicles, and with headlights off drove on the improvised path toward the highway. We waited a moment in the dark for the section of the road to clear of other vehicles. Then on cue, we turned our headlights on, mounted the asphalt stretch and started the long trip to the Red Sea.

It was a crazy ride. We floored the gas pedals. The condition of the roads in the Gedaref area was pretty good. Our biggest concern was running into the huge stones used by Sudanese drivers as improvised warning markers. Because dimming of headlights is an uncommon practice in Sudan, each time a heavy truck came toward us, we drove completely blinded by the glare of the oncoming headlights.

Danny led the way with the Toyota laden with equipment and no passengers. This allowed him to move at relatively high speed. Marcel followed in the pickup carrying dozens of Jews in its cargo hold, whose cumulative weight put the rear axle under stress Toyota engineers had never dreamed of. By contrast, the truck's nose was almost sailing in the air. "What a god-awful thing," Marcel said. "All I need now is a flat tire."

The two trucks crammed full of passengers brought up the rear.

Having survived the pick-up, we faced the task of transporting hundreds of Jews across hundreds of kilometers, studded at nearly every junction with a police or military control point, which we had been able to pinpoint thanks to earlier reconnaissance.

A typical checkpoint was made up of a row of oil drums across the road and between them a narrow passage manned by a policeman or a sleepy soldier, sometimes two. The officer in charge and the rest of the soldiers were sitting in a rickety shack by the roadside.

Danny served as "checkpoint monitor." A few kilometers ahead of the first checkpoint, he would race the pickup truck toward the control point. He stopped the vehicle nonchalantly, handed the soldiers cigarettes and knowing they were dying for rusks, which he described as *esh Fransawi* (French bread), he opened several boxes containing this delicacy. Amid idle talk about the weather and the gorgeous view, he explained to the officer in charge that the remainder of his vehicles would turn up within minutes, which sure enough they did. "Here they are," he told the officer, pointing at us and signaling to us, as if he were in charge, to clear the roadblock and continue ahead.

That was our method for going through roadblocks — a simple exercise, without unnecessary sophistication, which proved effective.

"And what do we do if they demand that we stop?" Danny was asked during a briefing.

"If the soldier merely checks the papers, no sweat. But if he starts climbing over the side to see what's inside, you should hit the gas pedal and disappear. By the time the soldiers get over the incident, you'll be far away."

"And what do we do if the soldiers climb into their jeep and start chasing us?" "It's more than likely that the jeep starter won't work, and by the time they begin to jump-start the jeep, you will be far away. If they catch up with us, the last truck will try to push the jeep off the road. We've got to pray that: (a) we don't reach such a situation, and (b) that if it does happen, their communications won't work, or else we'll truly be in trouble..."

The cigarette and *esh Fransawi* routine worked like a charm for all checkpoints: Shawak, Khashim el Gerba, Atbara Bridge, Kassala, Aroma, Sinkat and Suakin, except for one serious mishap. At one of the roadblocks, due both to fatigue and the condition of the vehicles, we caused a pileup. The overburdened pickup truck hit a barrel and sent it flying away. The truck behind it managed to brake, but the truck in the rear rammed into it and shoved it towards the pickup truck.

The troops manning the roadblock were in shock. We too. We were certain that hysterical screams would rise within seconds from the cargo boxes, but there wasn't a squeak from the trucks or the pickup truck.

We were first to come round. We waved the soldiers off, as if a pileup in the center of a police roadblock was part of our regular driving routine, and soon blended with the darkness.

We pulled up after several kilometers of wild driving. Dr. Pomeranz, the doctor in the group, hastened to climb over the boxes to check on the passengers. Hundreds of eyes followed him with fear and concern.

"No. No one was hurt," the head of the groups told us. Dr. Pomeranz scanned them quickly, to reach the same conclusion: "It seems that the force of impact was lessened due to the crowding. All's well."

A quick survey of the vehicles revealed that they, too, suffered no substantial damage, except for a slight bend on the accelerator pedal of one of the pickup trucks. We soon overcame the problem and continued driving, until a pale strip began marking the spot in the east where the great wheel of the sun would soon emerge. Danny's pickup truck left the road. We followed, driving on for several kilometers along a narrow trail into a wadi which could not be seen from the road.

Tense and fatigued, we stopped the vehicles and let down their side panels. We started counting the alighting passengers who looked weak but smiled nevertheless. Unbelievable: 175 men, women, babies and elderly people! An entire small village packed into two trucks and a small pickup truck.

We quickly got organized for a day's stay in the wadi. Assisted by younger members of the group we distributed water, rusks and whatever fruit and vegetables we had. The interpreter emphasized to the group that they were forbidden to spread out over the area. In case of emergency, for example, being discovered by passersby, we would have to clear the area within minutes. "Try to rest, because we will be continuing on our way during the night," the group leaders told their people.

The remote wadi, which probably isn't marked on any map, started teeming with life. After hours of standing in the crowded vehicles, the "brothers" were happy to stretch their limbs, later preparing for a stay in the area. There were no trees in the wadi, only a small number of bushes and large rocks in whose shade they gathered by individual families, erecting improvised tents from blankets and cloth kerchiefs.

It was actually our first chance to see our passengers up close. Their clothing showed want and poverty. Most of the women wore traditional white dresses and large head scarves. The wardrobe also included several other multipurpose white cloth kerchiefs, which they used for bundling babies, packing the few belongings they had and for making the improvised tents.

The men's fashion was divided into three styles: the elderly wore broad traditional robes and carried a cane, which served not just for support but also as a symbol of authority. The younger adults wore European-type clothing — a frayed jacket and trousers that had seen better days. Some wore shoes without socks, and most had sandals on their feet. The younger set looked just like other young people anywhere in the world: jeans, T-shirts in myriad colors embossed with images of the Beatles or Coca Cola logos. There were cotton shirts too, carrying advertising promos — God only knows how they had reached East Africa — such as "Volunteer Firemen's Day, Hoff, Bavaria, June 1979."

A few dozen meters from the men and the children, several girls and women gathered in the shade of a large rock. Asked why they were sitting so far away, one of the young people told us that under the strict cleanliness codes observed by Ethiopian Jews, menstruating women may not stay with the rest of the community. "In Ethiopia you can see outside any village a special bungalow where they spend the unclean days away from the rest of the congregation," he explained in broken English. Even he didn't realize we were Israelis. Uri, Ferede and Danny told them that we were mercenaries of sorts who were transporting them to safety. Truth be said, we also looked the part — a bunch of filthy, unshaven white people, with dusty hair and hands black with grease. For this reason the adults kept their distance from us.

Dr. Shlomo Pomeranz went among them to make sure that none were seriously ill. From his past experience he knew that the refugees' state of health was poor, and besides disease stemming from the ravages of travel they also suffered from African diseases ranging from meningitis to malaria. AIDS was not yet known. After the medical examination he rolled up his sleeves and turned to his favorite hobby: greasing truck engines and changing oil.

We used the daytime hours for rest, refueling and playing with the children.

Children. Even in the midst of their adventurous ride on the way to freedom, the children remained children. After surveying their immediate scene they started, unlike the adults, to approach and study us.

After my years of work in Sudan, I'm no longer objective about anything pertaining to Ethiopian Jews. I admire them, their inner calm and the stamina that enabled them to stand up to terrible hardships on their way to freedom. It is the stamina of heroes. And their smiles — the sound of laughter of Ethiopian children has a unique sound. I heard it for the first time in that remote wadi somewhere in eastern Sudan.

Our conversations with them, with the help of hand gestures and pantomime, were flowing nonetheless. When we let them sit in the driver's cabin and touch the wheel, they were in seventh heaven. It was amazing to see how happy they were at sharing a piece of chewing gum among twenty children. They looked at us as though we were creatures from outer space.

Only some time later did we realize that for most of them it was the first time they had seen white people at such close range. We asked some for their names. Ethiopian names have a special ring, and I must admit that they did not register with me, perhaps due to fatigue and tension about the next phase of the operation. Anyway, I don't have a musical ear, which my neighbors in Tel Aviv can bear witness to, having suffered for two years through my failed attempt to play the saxophone.

Two years after this operation, when I had already left the unit and started working for *Maariv*, I was invited with a few other Hafisniks to a tour of an immigrant hostel in Atlit. The story of the exodus of Ethiopian Jews was still a closely held secret, and due to the military censor's blue pencil, had been kept from the general public. But in the communities where hostels were set up, such as Ashkelon, Afula and Atlit, all the veteran residents knew that these were immigrants from Ethiopia. At the time, the Ethiopians still received a warm welcome. The problems of racial prejudice cropped up later. "How do I get to the immigrant hostel?" our minibus driver asked at the entrance to Atlit. "Ah, you're looking for the black ones? Drive straight ahead to the end of the street and then turn right…"

That day was a nice winter day. We were introduced to the center management as Jewish Agency employees. An adult Hebrew class was taking place on the lawn. Their faces read despair. These people were cut off from their country of birth and had come to a new place, which received them with open arms, but at the same time heaped no few obstacles on their way to integration. In addition, they had to learn a new and very difficult language.

To the side, some children were playing soccer, cheering in Amharic and Hebrew. The children noticed us right away, and one of them with curly hair, huge eyes and a disarming smile studied us carefully. Suddenly he came close, caught my hand and said in good Hebrew: "Uncle, I remember you from the red truck in the wadi." I must confess: I cried.

A part of the local team of the Arous Village, Sudan.

The dining room in the village.

The village team, all Mossad people under cover as tourist experts, preparing the rowboat for a maritime tour with the guests.

The author and a photo of Sudan's leader, General Jaafar Nimeiri.

Broadcasting from the middle of the desert, on our trucks, to headquarters in Israel; the antenna is stretched, the time is appropriate…transmitting…

The Khartoum Hilton, an island of prosperity in a sea of poverty and despair.

Dr. Shlomo Pomerantz, the devoted and brave doctor, taking care of our Japanese Hino truck in the middle of the desert.

Waiting in the desert to begin an operation.

Robi with a smuggler's boat in the background. We have an unwritten
agreement with the smugglers: "live and let live"; we don't bother them
and they don't bother us.

Desert mobility, Sudanese style: barrels of fuel and water, spare wheels,
metal anti-theft cage.

The Israeli naval commando on his way to a meeting with the Mossad people on the Sudanese shore.

Preparing to mark a landing beach.

Removing the commando rowboats from the *Bat Galim*.

Young Jewish women on their way from Ethiopia to Israel via Sudan.

An honorary plaque that was given to the participants of the operation to rescue Ethiopia's Jews from Sudan; Gadash is the author's nickname (photograph by Eli Dasa).

Chapter 23

Soon after nightfall we set out on the last leg of the overland voyage. Altogether the operation had gone according to planning and expectations. We cleared the roadblocks without difficulty and bypassed Port Sudan without getting mired in the marshes.

We made it to the rendezvous point with the Navy SEALs. Coordination at the meet was carried out in English, of course. When the navy boat emerged from the darkness, I suddenly heard a question in Hebrew. "Which one here is Shimron?" It was the voice of Gadi Sukenik. At the end of the 1970s, after my first stint with the Mossad, I returned to work for a year with Kol Israel (Israel radio). And there I met Sukenik. He was then a cub reporter with the radio's current affairs department and also a Navy SEAL reservist. Three years had gone by since our last meeting, but Sukenik, a radio man with a keen ear, immediately identified the voice blaring from the speaker of the communication radio opposite Sudan's hostile shoreline.

The handover of the "brothers" to the protecting hands of IDF soldiers went smoothly, too. Sailing toward the mother ship *INS Bat Galim* took about an hour and a half. A strong northerly wind of forty knots whipped up high waves. Many of the "brothers" vomited everything they had ever eaten. The army doctor on board one of the boats was forced to hook them up to IV drips several times during the tough sailing.

The initial planning called for the Zodiacs and their passengers to drive into the landing craft directly through the opening in the front. But because of the high waves and the danger of capsizing, the ship's captain came up with a makeshift solution: the boats were hoisted by cranes to the height of fifteen meters, and then lowered directly into the bowels of the boat.

The "brothers," cowering under sheets of tarpaulin that protected them from the waves, didn't understand what was going on.

The navy sailors said that only one elderly woman realized that it was not the way to board a boat. She started screaming and became hysterical. Only with great effort did they manage to calm her down with assistance from the Amharic-speaking escorts who were on board.

Two months later, during the next operation, everything was entirely different. It was a miracle that the operation did not end in terrible disaster, which if leaked to the press, would have provided an endless supply of banner headlines. But more about that later.

We returned to our village. Having received a congratulatory cable from headquarters over the brilliant execution, we started getting ready for a well-deserved rest and also improving the living conditions at the site.

First of all, we had to cross out the word Jaffa from the hundreds of oranges in the food crates left for us by the navy sailors as a free gift. We found consolation in the fact that the commanding officers of the *Bat Galim* had meant well. And that the oranges were superb.

Twenty-four hours of peace and quiet put us back on a routine course. Ruby, Shmulik, Dr. Pomeranz and Marcel went diving to explore the reefs in the area, and Danny and I went to Port Sudan to advance the cause of the Arous Holiday Village with the local authorities. "We must show the flag and leave signs that we are in the midst of legitimate tourist activity," Danny said.

Our first mission was to meet the Sudanese Danny had named in the fall as the Navco company representative in the city. He waited for us at his home, a sumptuous villa by local standards, on the outskirts of the city.

He was a very good-looking man, tall, about fifty years old, extraordinarily suspicious, clever and greedy. The last trait eclipsed the others. We imagined that he suspected our intentions and had asked himself why, despite the many months that had gone by since his nomination as company rep, not a single tourist had arrived in the area. In addition, he was also sexually frustrated: he had evidently cultivated high expectations about the incredible time he would have in the village with the hundreds of shapely, golden-haired female tourists who were expected to land in Port Sudan in droves. Therefore, it was important for us to impress upon him that Navco was gearing itself up for thriving commercial activity. We showered him with soothing explanations, to the effect that this kind of business develops very slowly. This business chat was the strangest I had ever had.

The Sudanese lay a large whiskey bottle on the table and exhorted us to drink. He himself sat on a sofa with floral upholstery, holding a fleshy Eritrean prostitute in each arm. The two caressed him endlessly, kissed him on the eyes and lips, ran their fingers through his hair, and occasionally inserted their hands under the white galabiyeh he was wearing, mimicking what they saw on a large television screen that was placed in front of them. The TV set was hooked up to an outsized and outdated video cassette recorder playing a highly explicit porno movie. The bold images were accompanied by a booming dialogue in basic German which could be understood without German language classes: "*Schnell, schnell, ja, so ist gut* (quick, yes, that is good)," and so on and so forth.

And as if this was not enough, our Sudanese host had been smoking hashish — the odor was still wafting in the room as we entered.

Everything blended that evening to make the Sudanese an exemplary host, charming, generous and oozing promises to move heaven and earth for us: recruit contractors, hire workers, intercede with the authorities to improve the access route to the village. Everything we asked for produced a solemn promise for speedy execution accompanied by a fist thump on the solar plexus for extra conviction. He had no complaint whatsoever, except for a minor request for "an advance of a few thousand Sudanese pounds."

"At this stage this bum doesn't suspect anything," Danny said as we departed, having left the Sudanese a not-too-large sum of money. "It'd be foolish to make an enemy of him over a few hundred pounds. His contacts are too good."

That day, we also called on the city governor, the commander of the navy and several merchants. We dispensed smiles and promises everywhere and left small sums of money in the right hands as a "donation to the local orphanage," a near official modifier throughout the Third World for the slush fund of the local powermonger, in order to ensure industrial quiet.

After settling things down and following a brief R & R period, Danny, Marcel, Shlomo Pomeranz and Shmulik flew to Khartoum to the civilized ambience of the Hilton, and from there to Europe, promising to see us again during the next operation.

Chapter 24

Danny instructed Ruby and me "to do everything to spruce up the village and prepare it to receive tourists." How to do it was something neither he nor we quite knew. And therefore we did our best.

In Port Sudan we located an electricity and refrigeration technician, touted by the locals as "the best between here and Khartoum." We brought him to the village. He was an amiable Egyptian Copt, armed with a large toolbox. Inside a week he managed to refurbish some air conditioners for partial use. He also improvised a new electrical grid that withstood the fluctuating load of our generator for about a week. On the eighth day it crashed, almost killing us.

One evening, within minutes, a dense black cloud cover hid the skies and driving rain of the desert variety — each drop the size of a lake — came down on our heads.

The uppermost layer of sand became sealed within seconds and turned the plateau on which the village was built into a huge swamp. At the center was the junction box that our Coptic electrician contractor had devised. Ali the driver, also in charge of the generators, proved his loyalty by running in the driving rain to the generator shack.

Promptly at five, per standing orders, he turned on the generator. The flash of light that burst from the junction box the second Ali hooked the generator to the grid was the brightest I had ever seen. If a spy satellite happened to pass over the area, there is no doubt that its highly sensitive equipment recorded the flash. And if this indeed happened, then NSA code crackers are probably still wondering what in hell was the bright light that flashed suddenly in the Port Sudan area in early 1982 — perhaps a repeat of an explosion recorded in 1979 in Prince Edward Island south of Cape Town that raised speculation about a joint Israeli-South African nuclear experiment. I am happy to offer an alternative solution. A tongue of fire leapt from the junction box, and a spark raced along the cable laid by the contractor, reached the second junction box next to the dining hall, and then died in a clap of thunder.

The fact that on the way to the dining hall the spark hurt none of the residents and that all of us escaped unharmed from this episode was just one item on a long list of tiny miracles that occurred during this operation.

Besides the electrical contractor, we brought in a building contractor from the city, a plump Sudanese, to take charge of refurbishment of the rooms in the village. The contractor, like most Sudanese, was an amiable man who liked to joke and, as it transpired later on, was completely devoid of concerns and fears, or perhaps he should be described as a "fearless fool."

One day, when Ruby and I returned to the village from a routine sortie to the coral reefs in the open sea, the contractor was waiting for us on the improvised pier, close to the diving equipment storeroom. "May I perhaps borrow a mask, snorkel and fins?" he asked. "I have heard so much about the beautiful fish and corals living here, and I have never had a chance to see them up close."

We were glad to accommodate him. Asked if he knew how to use a mask and a snorkel, he responded with confidence: "No problem."

To be on the safe side, I decided to stick with him, should he need an explanation nonetheless.

The contractor took off his clothes, revealing a tight bathing suit under a respectable stomach. He managed somehow to put the fins on, but drew a blank with the mask. His particularly long nose got crushed inside the mask, and vapors started building up on the lenses. I showed him how to use saliva to wipe off the lenses and how to attach the snorkel. He tried to walk forward, but forgot that he had fins on his feet. His first step thus ended with a clumsy roll on the beach. But giving up was no option for such an obstinate character. He rose to his feet and entered the water in reverse with a faltering step, resembling a penguin walking in a film screened backwards.

The section of the beach the contractor decided to dip in was characterized by a sheer drop. A meter away from the shoreline, it was impossible to stand. When the water level reached the height of his knees, he waved that everything was well. A second later, he disappeared.

It took some time before I realized that something had gone very wrong.

The contractor vanished completely — not even the tip of his snorkel could be seen above water. As I was pondering the developments, the head of our contractor shot up like a torpedo launched in the depths, his arms flailing like the wings of a Dutch windmill in a storm, and his mouth producing stifled cries. In short, he appeared to be in an advanced state of drowning.

Within seconds I reached him and pulled him to the shore. The mask on his face was full of seawater. A quarter of the snorkel's length was shoved deep into his mouth, including the rubber guard that your average diver keeps in the general area of his teeth. Strange gurgling noises were coming out of his mouth. He recovered after several moments of retching and severe coughing.

"Never in my life was I in the water and I can't swim," he admitted.

"Why didn't you tell us? We would have shown you how or given you floats."

"It looked so simple on TV," he said with childish innocence. "I was sure that I go into the water, and that's that."

The contractor's brief sortie into the water of the Red Sea made Abu Medina very happy. Abu Medina was the eldest of our workers, a fisherman with hawk's eyes and an amazing sense of orientation, as well as an insatiable womanizer. There was no match for him across the region for locating interesting reefs or identifying the exact location of exotic shipwrecks worth diving onto. Abu Medina, who preferred being called The Spirit of Arous, was away when we arrived in the village the first time. But one day, after hearing that the *hawaja*, the foreign masters, were back in Arous, he promptly reported to work.

Abu Medina simply could not tolerate the urban Sudanese of the contractor's type, perhaps due to residual pride of the local people, descendants of Bedouin, who controlled the sea lanes in the past and now were reduced to second-class citizens in a state whose leadership was composed of urban people, represented by the contractor. It was thus that when the contractor began choking because of the water in his lungs, Abu Medina, who was standing near the boat gear shed and witnessed the incident, broke into a series of joyful giggles. But a minor case of swallowing the wrong way, on top of his health and breathing problems, turned Abu Medina's laughter into ominous gurgles.

The contractor had fully recovered in the meantime. It must be said to his credit that he promptly enlisted in the effort to save Abu Medina, which mostly included strong slaps on the back, until The Spirit of Arous resumed normal breathing.

Abu Medina was quick to repay the kindness, by helping the contractor realize his dream to take a look at the Red Sea world of silence. He went to the equipment shed and took out a plastic bucket with a glass bottom, which we called a "poor people's glass-bottomed boat," or the "Sudanese Shooftoscope" — a hybrid of the Arabic word *shoof* (to see), and telescope. The contractor had to do nothing but sit comfortably in the boat, immerse the bucket in the water and look at the fish.

The term *Shooftoscope* is an example of the expansion of the local dialect with new words that entered the language due to the clandestine sojourn of the Israelis in the Port Sudan area between the years 1981 and 1985.

Our employees wanted to learn English and fast. They were certain that within a few weeks the place would be crawling with tourists from all over the world. Throughout the day, they asked us to name the English word for anything they pointed at. In most cases, the answers conformed to the definitions in the Oxford dictionary of the English language. But sometimes we had to invent words, which of all things penetrated the local dialect. To wit: one day Abu Medina pointed at a funnel used to refuel the boat engines and asked what it was called in English. None of us could think at the moment of the word *funnel* and so we came up with an improvisation: *mashpechino* (a combination of the Hebrew word for funnel, *mashpech*, and an Italian-sounding suffix). The locals who still remembered the Italian era at Arous immediately fell in love with the "new" English word with the rolling sound and promptly adopted it. After that, a request along the lines of "Mohammed, please hand me the mashpechino" was pretty common and understandable.

One Friday Danny felt a strong craving for some Yiddishkeit (Jewish culture). He went to Chief Cook Moussa, who was in charge of baking bread and rolls, and explained to him what a *challah* (special bread for the Sabbath) looked like. That same evening, Moussa brought a properly baked, braided *challah* to the table. Hassan said the *challah* reminded him of *Shabbat*, a sandal in Sudanese. What a coincidence. Moussa's festive bread was promptly named "Shabbatcake." Several Sudanese thus learned that the special cake was used to designate the beginning of the weekend which was so important to the Europeans. But they had no explanation as to what cake had to do with a sandal.

I would not be surprised, either, if in some popular eateries in Port Sudan a customer ordered *dakim-dakim* french fries. This new term penetrated the local language after we got tired of eating Moussa's thick potato sticks. "This is how we want them," we demonstrated by bringing our fingers close together, "*dakim-dakim* ('thin-thin' in Hebrew)."

And there was also the word *mashehu-mashehu* to denote something exceptional. Articulated with a thin voice, it assumed a Chinese ring. Ali the driver lovingly adopted the phrase *ein davar* ("never mind" in Hebrew). You can imagine the surprise of the new crew members who traveled with him for the first time along the potholed road from Port Sudan Airport to the village, when they heard him say with each bump "*ein davar*" between his teeth.

Chapter 25

A week after Danny and his team returned to Israel, the following message was picked up in the village: "Following the success of the naval operation, it was decided to adopt this mode of action in future operations to rescue 'brothers' from Sudan.

"Therefore it has been decided to earmark an appropriate budget and invest more efforts in renovating the village to strengthen the tourist infrastructure that allows us freedom of movement across Sudan. Already in the next few days we shall send you a hotel and food consultant who will be responsible for the functioning of the village and its adaptation to the new standard."

Ruby and I were very happy with the wise decision from headquarters, especially due to the fact that it gave us a few extra days to exploit to the utmost the life of serenity and nirvana at the place.

We now let Bedouism take us over completely. And since it was getting hotter and hotter by the day, any message that removed the last shreds of responsibility or burden off our shoulders was gladly received. We sank into a blessed R & R routine that included a permanent ritual of popping anti-malaria pills, good sleep, a lot of sports and plenty of food.

One day this routine was interrupted when one of my teeth was broken by a small stone that mixed in with the rice prepared by Chief Cook Moussa.

I was in great pain, which in civilized society would have been easily relieved by a visit to a trained dentist. But in such a remote place as the Arous Holiday Village, in an enemy country where you're living under assumed identity, a mundane problem like severe tooth pain is hard to solve.

I got on the pickup truck and drove to Port Sudan. I took with me a sheaf of banknotes and documents and told Ruby that if I didn't return by evening, it would indicate that my condition had gotten worse and I had gotten on a flight to Khartoum in the hope of finding a decent dentist.

In Port Sudan I was directed to the government hospital at the edge of the city. Except for several trees and remnants of a lawn in the center, the hospital looked like a replica of the security forces camp in Gedaref, where Ruby and I had spent a few difficult hours several weeks earlier.

Hundreds of civilians moved slowly between the bungalows, some ill and others, mostly relatives of patients, simply depending on the hospital for their food and well-being. I asked a man in a robe that had long lost its original whiteness to direct me to the *mudir* (manager).

The *mudir*, an extremely hospitable fifty-year-old who spoke fluent English, was glad to see me. Yes, he had heard about the Arous Holiday Village, and that a European company was operating the site again, and naturally he would be happy to help us when in need.

Despite the pain I decided to seize on his generosity and his sincere desire to help, to look into another matter that pertained to the operation of the village, and asked him if he happened to know if there was a pressure chamber for treating diving accident victims anywhere. He broke into uproarious laughter. "There is no pressure chamber between Suez and Aden. Though the French navy in Djibouti might have one," he said, absentmindedly volunteering a piece of important intelligence — that members of the Sudanese naval frogmen, stationed in the military section of the Port Sudan harbor, had probably not done any diving because of gear maintenance problems.

I then presented my broken tooth problem to him. "You are extremely lucky," he said. "Our dentist is a fine professional. Come along, I'll take you to him."

Some twenty men and women waited on the balcony at the entrance to the dentistry department. They all rose up in awe at the sight of the *mudir* and his guest. Without knocking on the door, the *mudir* went into the room dragging me in tow.

The treatment room looked like a Western dentist's nightmare. It was a large space, with window openings lacking glass panes or screens. In the center, under a large fan, which of course was not functioning, stood a swivel chair with a back, of the kind that was obligatory in men's barbershops in the 1930s. The dentist's equipment included a hand drill resembling an amateur Black and Decker drill, converted for dental use. There was a small metal cabinet with shelves displaying several packets of cotton wool and a box of blades and bits. A decorated diploma from the dental school of the University of Alexandria hung on the wall.

Dr. Ossman — that was his name to the best of my recall — wearing a robe in the once-white color that appeared to be the de rigueur fashion of this establishment, hastened to clear the chair. He sent the patient who was sitting there when we came in, a local old woman who was whimpering from her near toothless mouth, out of the room promising to continue her treatment "later."

"The situation is not so simple," he said in fairly good English after a thorough look at my jaws. "The tooth broke because of infection that built up under its gold inlay. I will have to remove the inlay, clean the area and rebuild your tooth."

Did I have a choice? I knew that the University of Alexandria enjoyed a good reputation, at least in Egypt.

Dr. Ossman worked alone, without assistants. Next to my lips he placed a stainless steel bowl of a type that can be seen today only in old movies and dental medicine museums, which was intended to hold the saliva that was oozing from my mouth. They obviously didn't have suction hoses anywhere in Port Sudan. For an anesthetic he used the same spray applied to football players writhing with pain from injuries suffered during play.

"It'll hurt," he warned. "But I work quickly and efficiently."

I shut my eyes, cursing the moment I had volunteered to go to Sudan, and opened my mouth. The nightmare in the dental clinic of Port Sudan Hospital took more than an hour, because it also included an electrical power failure.

The pain was horrible. Years later I watched the movie *The Marathon Man*, which deals with a young Jewish man, portrayed by Dustin Hoffman, who inadvertently gets on the trail of a fugitive Nazi criminal who had been a cruel concentration camp doctor, portrayed by Sir Lawrence Olivier. At one point the Nazi manages to capture the Jew and tries to get information out of him. Hoffman remains silent, and then the Nazi, also qualified as a dentist, shifts to a sick torture method: he drills holes in Hoffman's teeth, without any anesthetic of course.

I recall being physically uncomfortable during the screening. I'm convinced that I was the only spectator in the auditorium who was familiar with the pain the scriptwriter was trying to convey. "Are you not feeling well?" asked my female companion to the movie, seeing the beads of sweat rolling down my face and hearing my quickened breathing.

"That's it," Dr. Ossman announced with satisfaction. "I glued the inlay back in. It looks like new."

I warmly shook his hand, and asked how much I owed him.

"Oh, no. We are a socialist country. The treatment is without charge," he said. We parted after an endless string of mumbled thanks.

While making my way slowly across the balcony toward the exit gate, with the tip of my tongue trying to assess Ossman's work, I heard the patter of flip-flops behind me. Dr. Ossman stopped me, panting. "It is a socialist state," he said. "But I would be happy if you paid me fifty pounds."

We went back to the treatment room and sheltered by the closed door I paid him fifty pounds for his work, which in retrospect proved to be superb.

"I don't know what the level of dentistry in Kenya is like, but whoever took care of this tooth did a super job," said my regular dentist who saw me immediately after my return to Israel, some two months later. I couldn't give the whole story about Ossman and his Black and Decker, and thus made up a story about a safari in Kenya.

Returning to the village I found Ruby practicing a new technique for suntanning the space between the toes, and quickly joined him, abandoning myself to sun-worship.

The routine remained pleasant. From time to time we supervised a small but necessary refurbishing job and graciously accommodated casual guests and passersby. One day, for instance, a reinforced Egyptian army platoon landed in our midst.

At the time, relations between Egypt and Sudan were particularly warm, and a joint military exercise for units of both armies was taking place in the area. At the end of the drill, a small Egyptian unit set out to tour the region and noticing the holiday village bungalows, popped in to visit. We let them use two dilapidated bungalows at the northern end of the village. Four amiable and smiling officers used the rooms, while the soldiers slept under the trucks.

The commander of the unit, a tall army major who spoke fluent English, gave his word of honor that he and his soldiers would leave the place as they found it and would not cause damage to property. To his credit, he was as good as his word.

They spent two days in the village, played football, dipped in the sea and ate fish. From time to time we went over to see how they were and to make sure they didn't empty out the rooms. They invited us to have tea with them and shoot the breeze.

I know Egypt well. I have visited there many times and in my opinion the Egyptians rank among the most likeable people in the world — warm, patient and able to retain a sense of humor even when caught in a Cairene traffic jam at 48 degrees (over 118 Fahrenheit) in the shade...where there is none available.

The officers, who naturally did not know that we were Israelis, went on and on about their brave exploits in the 1973 October War, noting that they had scored a "great victory over the boastful Israelis."

I couldn't help but smile. In the fall and winter of 1973–74 I did a long stint of reserve duty as an intelligence officer in "Africa," the patch of territory Israeli forces occupied west of the Suez Canal after the war. I was thoroughly familiar with Kilometer 101, Jebel Attaka, Jebel Genefa and Suez City. Then, I met face-to-face with Egyptian officers for the first time when we allowed supplies through to the besieged Egyptian Third Army with United Nations mediation. In no time, the meetings, which began on a note of mutual suspicion, revealed common characteristics: they too were reservists, from Cairo or Alexandria, patriots and entirely confident of the justice of their cause. In fact, all they wanted was to return home in one piece and live quietly thereafter. Even then I learned to appreciate the Egyptians' sense of humor, readily employed under any circumstances.

"See how our roles have reversed," an Egyptian officer told us on the banks of the canal. "Until 1967 we were based in the Sinai, along the Israeli border, rarely going home on furloughs, riding on buses for hours on end, busting our posteriors. We envied you Israelis, that it took you two hours in all to reach Tel Aviv. But now you must wander for hours through the entire Sinai, while we are an hour away from Cairo."

We smiled. "Yes, but you are stuck on the eastern side of the canal, with the IDF closing in on you from every direction. What furloughs are you talking about? See where you are."

The Egyptian broke into a booming laugh, gestured with his hand and winked as if he was about to disclose a state secret. He whispered: "Every day there is a furlough roster. We go home in a submarine…"

The Egyptian army major who was now a guest at our village had served in the Yom Kippur War in the Second Egyptian Army, the same army that penetrated northern Sinai and enabled then Egyptian president Anwar Sadat to claim the war as an Egyptian victory. The truth is that the Egyptian army lost the battle but Egypt won the war. Sadat achieved his goals: an Israeli army retreat from the waterline and the reopening of the Suez Canal, followed later by the return of the entire Sinai Peninsula to Egyptian sovereignty.

"The chapter with Israel is now closed," the officer said. "There is peace and our president, Sadat, the initiator of peace, only recently paid for it with his life. Very soon the Israelis will give up the last meter of Sinai…" Changing the subject, he said: "A curse be upon the Palestinians. President Sadat opened the door for them to accommodate the Israelis. But as usual, they are not prepared for any compromise. We are tired of them; we have fought against the Israelis four times and only because of those Palestinian ingrates."

I was not surprised at the officer's anti-Palestinian outburst — that was the prevailing mood at the time. When I visited Egypt, I spent an afternoon with a senior Egyptian personality over a bottle of whiskey. The afternoon turned into a long night. And as the level of drink in the bottle dropped below the halfway mark, he gave me his opinion of the Palestinian problem: "One Palestinian in the Nile — pollution. All the Palestinians in the Nile — solution."

Now I was hearing from this officer similar jokes about Palestinian obstinacy and diplomatic stupidity. Sitting in faraway Sudan, drinking hot tea, we did not know that at that very moment, a series of attacks against Israel was being planned at Abu Nidal's headquarters, including the assassination attempt on the Israeli ambassador to Britain. This murderous attack was the trigger for Israeli prime minister Menachem Begin to launch a war in Lebanon that took longer than planned and directly affected our operation.

The encounter with the Egyptian officers on the bank of the Red Sea broke the somewhat lazy routine Ruby and I had been keeping. Never had I eaten as much fish and seafood as during those days. Ruby continued diving from time to time, but in the meantime we discovered another source of fresh fish. A local fisherman who lived in a ramshackle bungalow on the far side of the lagoon brought us his catch every day. One day he sold us a giant lobster called in Sudanese Arabic *Sarsar*, for five dollars.

Ruby, a veteran sea dog, cooked the lobster in whiskey and other secret herbs and the outcome pleased our palates very much.

But the lobster was so big that we couldn't finish it. We offered to share with our workers but they ate no *Sarsar*.

We were a bit drunk and carefree. So we started throwing pieces of cooked lobster meat at each other accompanied by raucous laughter and Indian battle cries. It was a totally surrealistic picture, which I'm sure a Mossad psychologist would have loved to watch and analyze. It was then that we received a message from headquarters to go to Port Sudan and collect the man they were sending to run the village professionally. Besides the physical description we were given, we were advised of his nickname, which did not ring a bell with us.

We went to Port Sudan Airport, which resembled the Eilat airport in the 1950s: a runway, a post with a windsock, a makeshift control tower and an open shed. And who should get off the Boeing 737 airliner of Inshallah Airways (our nickname for Sudan Airways)? None other than Apke.

I knew Apke very well from the Mossad headquarters in Tel Aviv. He ran the big kitchen there, and like any other office crammed with bored workers, lunch was the centerpiece of the workday, affecting the division of the daily activity into "Before Food" and "After Food." This explained Apke's central role in the daily routine of anyone who made his living there.

Apke was now about fifty-five years old, short and round. Even his thick-lensed glasses could not hide the fiendish spark in his eyes. He certainly had experience and knowledge in the running of kitchens, but clandestine operations were completely outside his field of expertise.

I shook his hand warmly, but certainly didn't share my doubts with him about the wisdom of sending a person like him to a godforsaken place like Arous.

I suppressed the question that immediately suggested itself: "Why? Are you crazy? Coming here at your age and in your state of health?" I remembered his tales about his frequent visits to doctors back home. We put his suitcases in the vehicle and after taking him around Port Sudan, we set out on our way.

I believe that even during this first trip along a rough dirt road, forty kilometers (twenty-five miles) of bumps and dust, Apke must have realized that he had come to the wrong place.

When he saw the filth in the kitchen, he almost had a heart attack. But to his credit, it must be said that he recovered very quickly. "Take out pots, boil water, add soap and start scrubbing the walls," he shouted at Moussa and Mohammed. Hassan the waiter tried to dodge the assignment, insisting he was only a waiter and had no business between the burners, but found no sympathy. He was forced to join the "scrubbing commando" along with Ali the driver and the rest of the workers in the village.

Scrubbing noises arose from the kitchen for two days straight. But Apke was not mollified until the walls were bright and the pots shiny. I have no doubt that in those days the kitchen in Arous was the cleanest in this part of the Red Sea.

Apke's vast experience in the food business — he was a real hotshot — gave an immediate boost to our standard of living. Apke forced the cooks to enlarge the selection of dishes, paid special attention to how the food was dished out, and at the same time nixed any chance that any of us would come down with a fatal intestinal disease because of contaminated food.

In the evening, we sat on the beach, drinking cold beer and chatting aimlessly. "What a hole," sneered Apke one evening. "End of the world. I never thought that was the state of affairs here. But I don't regret for a moment that I came here. Not even for a second did I hesitate to lend a hand. You are young," he continued, "born in Israel and grown up into the reality of a Jewish state. But I spent the years of my youth in Auschwitz. I immigrated to Israel as an illegal immigrant, and therefore I feel that I'm doing a sacred job here."

Even confirmed cynics like Ruby and I became emotional over the realization of Apke's Zionist dream in the prairies of Sudan.

Chapter 26

January and February flew by and soon the village looked ready to take vacationers. Proof of that came from an eccentric Englishman who appeared at the village gates one day and presented himself as a newspaperman specializing in covering exotic sites.

I seem to recall that his name was Christopher. He displayed curiosity of the same kind that pushed another Christopher — Columbus — to sail across oceans and discover new continents. He kept asking questions of all kinds, tried to fish for details about our business background, who we were financed by, what kind of company it was, and an assortment of technical details. He was greatly bothered for instance by where the pipes leading from the toilets ended. It was only after he discovered a large septic tank built by the Italian technicians on the western edge of the village that he calmed down a bit. All the answers he received were entered in a small, thick notebook, which also detailed at what angle he took each frame with his sophisticated Pentax camera.

To most of his questions we had no answers and the few that we did only seemed to whet his desire to ask more and more. Already on his first day at the village, we raised the possibility that he had been dispatched by MI6, the British espionage agency, to find out who was behind the renewed activity in the picturesque Arous lagoon. Consequently we tried to keep him at a distance. We were not short of excuses, from refurbishing work at the generator shed to checking motors and gear at sea. And Apke, listed in the records as a foreign passport holder, assumed a hard-to-understand Teutonic accent. Thus, Christopher preferred to talk to our local employees.

Christopher's stay with us was cut short because of a minor

accident. When he went swimming armed with mask and flippers, he attempted to climb on a coral reef using a rope that dangled from the reef into the water. If indeed he were a journalist with vast experience covering exotic sites, he should have known that ropes are the preferred habitation of thousands of small mollusks, which have extremely sharp edges and secrete a poisonous substance. In short, Christopher came back from his dip with arms all bruised and lacerated. Within a few hours, his hands became swollen, his body temperature went up and he understood that he had to be evacuated to Port Sudan to be treated in the hospital.

Our parting from the "British spy" was particularly painful. Each and every one of us, in turn, warmly squeezed his injured hands, and he jumped with pain. We haven't heard from him since. To this day, I'm waiting to see the story he promised to publish and send on to us.

And so, we had several pleasant weeks between the end of January and early March 1982, while at Mossad headquarters, preparations were going on for another rescue operation.

The network of activists in the refugee camps, the Committee men, reported to Uri daily instances of Jews arriving from Ethiopia with tales of relentless persecution by neighbors and harassment by government officials. "Terrible tragedies are unfolding there all the time," said the reports to Mossad headquarters. "Highway bandits hit refugee convoys, rob, rape, pillage and murder. There is shortage of food and medicines. The refugees are victimized by the army and the police. Protection fees are collected. Aid shipments are being stolen. Sudanese police have received reports that there are Jews hiding among the refugees and rumors that Jews are managing to leave Sudan for Israel have begun circulating in the camps. Help!"

Danny again assembled a team of agents. One of them, Joe, was a veteran Mossad man, nearing retirement, a consummate technician with many exploits to his credit. His life story was complicated. At a young age, he was sent to live with a rich aunt in Paris, to absorb the French culture. A short while later, World War II broke out, and contact between Joe and his parents in Greece was cut off. After France's capitulation in June 1940, Joe endured a whole gamut of persecutions and wanderings. His aunt succeeded in placing him in a monastery, where he was brought up as a Christian. Only after the war was he reunited with his parents, who managed to flee Greece and immigrate to Israel.

And thus, sometime during March 1982 our forces received a boost. The local workers, confident that they were harbingers of mass arrivals of tourists, were disappointed once more when they noticed that all of us, Apke included, were getting ready for a long trip. The declared destination was Khartoum. This time the cover story was not "letting off steam in the company of Swedish nurses at the ICRC hospital in Kassala," but rather taking delivery of equipment for the village flown over from Europe. It was a pretty flimsy story, but we were reconciled to the fact that cover stories were not the strongest point of our covert mission in Sudan.

After more than two months of living in field conditions in our own village, returning to the Hilton was like a return to paradise for Ruby and myself: hot baths, a glass of chilled beer in a crowded bar with women among the patrons, a book and newspaper stand, a well-tended swimming pool and soft bedding changed daily. In short: America.

We used the time until we received the green light from head-quarters, including confirmation that the *INS Bat Galim*, camou-flaged as an innocent merchant vessel, was waiting at sea, to fix our vehicles and get them ready for the long voyage.

Joe, for instance, managed to solve the problem in the Toyota carburetors, which became clogged due to filthy fuel. He cut the hoses carrying fuel from the tanks to the carburetors and hooked up an additional filter. We now had only to stop every five hundred kilometers (three hundred miles), remove the filters, clean them with a strong puff of air and put them back in place. Simple and efficient.

The plan of operation was a copy of the previous one, with the addition of lessons learned. To avoid dangerous loitering in the area, which characterized the two days prior to the previous operation, it was decided that this time we should leave Khartoum around noon, in coordination with Uri, who was staying at the Hilton. At night, we were to collect the "brothers" from a pre-set rendezvous point in the Gedaref area, proceed toward the shoreline, and on the second night hand them over to the Navy SEALs in Marsa Finjab, north of our holiday village.

The first part of the operation ran beautifully, right to the pickup. Because of a series of communication problems, and perhaps also for fear of informers, only 172 "brothers" reached the abandoned quarry set for the rendezvous, even though we were prepared to handle larger numbers.

The disappointment was great. You must remember that any such operation involves endless difficulties and risks. From an operational point of view, there was no great difference between picking up one hundred people or four hundred. Was it desirable to delay the pickup by one day to enable members of the Committee to gather more refugees? And if so, what to do with those who had already arrived after leaving all their property behind? Tell them to return to their shacks and come back the following day? Risky. They could have been spotted by neighbors who might have already informed the police. A brief police inquiry, certain to include threats and beatings, would expose the rendezvous set for the following night. This was our standing nightmare: policemen storming the vehicles shouting or even firing their weapons.

"A hundred seventy-two 'brothers' is not ideal, but that's what there is," Danny said. "Any other option will put the 'brothers' and ourselves at unnecessary risk. On our way!"

The long ride from Gedaref, through Kassala, Aroma and Sinkat passed uneventfully. The roadblocks were breached by the well-tried method, with Danny dispensing *esh Fransawi* and cigarettes to policemen.

About one hundred kilometers (sixty miles) from the Red Sea shoreline the road cuts through a 1,500-meter-high (5000-foot) mountain range. Our small convoy hid at the foot of the mountain range during the day. It was there that Ruby and I broke away from the convoy, but not before a new tactic was decided on: instead of transporting the "brothers" to the naval SEAL boats at sea, the boats would beach and they would board there.

The change was decided on after Defense Minister Ariel Sharon heard that previous operations had proceeded without a hitch, away from hostile eyes, and no longer feared an armed encounter between IDF soldiers and Sudanese troops, with all its complications. Our task was to reach the village as quickly as we could, put to sea in a Zodiac, mark the entry to Marsa Finjab with stick lights, survey the beach and lead the naval boats to it.

We reached the village in the afternoon, exhausted. Our loyal workers, who had gotten accustomed to our comings and goings, were happy to see us again, particularly after learning that the rest of the team was coming soon. After a hefty meal that included *dakim-dakim* french fries prepared by Chief Cook Moussa, Hassan asked us to help him solve some problems that had arisen during our absence. "Not now, Hassan," we told him mildly. "We want to go out for a little dive." If Hassan ever needed proof that we were crazy, it was borne out by our great desire to view the Red Sea treasures so shortly after a backbreaking trip from Khartoum.

"*Mejanin*, crazy," I heard him muttering.

Chapter 27

Night came quickly.

The gear was ready, but we rechecked it anyway: Zodiac, Mercury outboard motor, full tank of fuel, oars for emergencies, a bundle of light sticks, pocket flashlights, communication equipment and field glasses.

Because of the cold, each put on a windbreaker over our diving suits before we put to sea. The first task was to mark the winding entry route with light sticks, through the reefs, up to the *marsa* (lagoon) that was designated as a boarding point for the "brothers."

The moon had yet to appear, but the night was clear, without clouds, and visibility was reasonable. The sea was calm, slightly ruffled by a gentle breeze.

A first-class navigator, Ruby reached the first mark within minutes: a thin metal rod, dating to the days of the British, anchored in a concrete base and sticking a few centimeters above water. The reefs close by had dozens of similar metal rods. Past experience with boats running aground and damaging their motors proved that the access routes had to be marked more clearly, hence the decision to use light sticks.

To accustom fishermen in the area to the light sticks phenomenon, we started hooking them up in a few sites several weeks before the operation started, while spreading rumors that this was the way night-diving sites in Europe are marked.

A light stick is a plastic tube full of a chemical solution encasing a glass ampoule containing a different solution. When the tube is bent, the ampoule breaks and the chemical reaction between the two substances creates a bright green light that can last up to twenty hours.

Attaching the light sticks to the old metal rods was ostensibly a simple matter of tying them with a string. Ruby piloted the Zodiac carefully toward the reef. There was clearance of about thirty centimeters (around a foot) above the reef and the coral, which allowed the front of the boat to float through, but not the propeller shaft, which was immersed in the water. I stood on the bow, holding a light stick with a string attached at the top. I directed Ruby to the rod, whose base was anchored underwater, up to a distance that enabled me to clutch its base with my hand.

With one hand on the throttle and the other holding a powerful torch, Ruby illuminated the top of the rod.

Two points of light shone at us from the top of the rod and beneath them protruded the thick, strong beak of a suspicious adult osprey. The osprey is a bird of prey that feeds on fish. It is considered an endangered species. The word in Khartoum is that in Europe there are crazy collectors who are prepared to pay hundreds of dollars for a single osprey egg.

The area where the village was located is one of the few remaining havens for the bird, which is considered one of the most beautiful raptors among water birds. During the first days of our stay in the area, we discovered tens of osprey nests on a small island north of our lagoon. We spent hours watching their elegant flight — they have a wing span of over two meters — over the clear water of the Red Sea. When an osprey detects potential prey, it pulls its huge wings together and dives down like a Stuka — a Nazi Junkers 87 — although without the horrible whistle that characterized those murderous warplanes. Popular belief has it that an osprey catches fish with its strong curved beak. But in fact, it sinks its talons into the fish and transports it to its nest, appearing to an onlooker like an aircraft carrying a torpedo.

More to the point for me at the moment was the fact that an osprey can easily tear a piece of flesh off of an unprotected hand, because now one of these ospreys was looking down at me from a height of a few dozen centimeters with my hands almost touching its talons, and my body leaning at a forty-five-degree angle between the rod and the boat. Tales I read with horror as a child, descriptions of eye-picking eagles, erupted at once from the recesses of my gray cells into my consciousness.

"Go away!" I shouted at the osprey in English, as if the most important thing at the moment was to preserve my cover story... To be on the safe side, I added an angry gurgle like a hungry cat.

The osprey looked at me with diffidence, as if saying, "What's this thing disturbing the calm of my night?"

I repeated the shout, this time in Hebrew, adding a curse in Arabic and an assortment of other sounds.

Its reaction did not change, except for a movement that seemed to me to be a warning of imminent use of the talon option.

Ruby, who flashed his torch at the osprey, broke out in a ringing laughter at the image that Fellini himself could not have conceived for the craziest of his films: a single-minded osprey declaring war on two Mossad operatives on a covert mission.

Ruby let go of the throttle and the boat slid backward. At the same time the distance between my legs on the bow and my hand holding the base of the rod increased, pulling me to just a few centimeters from the osprey talons. Thus, hanging between the rod and the bow, between the danger of being punctured and a nasty fall over sharp-edged reefs, I shouted at Ruby, "I'm falling, hit the throttle full forward!"

Ruby came round, leaned on the throttle and the Zodiac sped forward. The bow got stuck on the concrete base of the rod. The propeller hit the side of the reef and started producing protest noises and clouds of coral dust.

This activity, plus the sudden and unusual noise, evidently got on the osprey's normally cool nerves. He took a hungry look at my fingers holding on to the rod, perhaps wondering if he should not make a tiny peck at the white flesh, but reconsidered seconds later, spread his huge wings and disappeared in a majestic glide into the night.

Weeks later, lounging at the Khartoum Hilton poolside, I saw

Ruby cutting an article from a newspaper. After scribbling a few words on it, he handed it to me ceremoniously. The article, from a Saudi Arabian newspaper in English, dealt with the osprey population in the Red Sea. "In memory of the Night of the Osprey" was the dedication he wrote on it for me.

Chapter 28

The marking of the access route into the lagoon proceeded peacefully. Quickly sailing from point to point, we attached the light sticks to the pre-chosen British-era rods, leaving our radio channels open. Except for static, no noise came out at all. We still had not picked up the members of Danny's group, who we knew were going around Port Sudan, but we weren't worried, because the range on our radio was limited to a few kilometers. In an emergency, the *Bat Galim* transmitter was to have served as a relay.

Three kilometers (a little under two miles) from the rendezvous point on the shore, close to a long reef, we suddenly noticed a big shadow. A quick look through the binoculars indicated that there was uninvited company.

"Hell, smugglers. They found themselves a place to anchor," was our joint diagnosis. It was a wooden boat typical of the area, about twenty meters long, topped by a single sail, a raised rear end and a diesel motor. Such a boat usually had a crew of up to five sailors.

The entire coastal strip from Port Sudan northward was a favored smuggling arena. Beyond the horizon lay rich Saudi Arabia, and on the Sudanese side, hundreds of kilometers of deserted shore replete with inlets offered countless opportunities for smuggling, particularly in view of the fact that Sudanese navy vessels seldom went out on patrols because of maintenance problems, a shortage of fuel, and perhaps fear of hitting the reefs. There were very few army patrols along the shore.

The Saudi market was happy to absorb the sheep and goats raised on the Sudanese side, and on the rebound the smugglers would bring consumer items that were hard to come by in Sudan. In the few months since our settling down in the holiday village, a "live and let live" policy shaped up between the smugglers and us. They gave up on Marsa Arous and moved over to other *marsas* like Darur, Awatir, Finjab, and others which are not even listed on the map.

From time to time we would find the body of a sheep that apparently had rolled off a smugglers' boat. One evening, apparently due to their captain's navigational error, a smugglers' boat ran aground directly opposite our village, about three hundred meters off shore. We followed with interest the rescue efforts of the crew, who very soon realized that we were watching them out of sheer curiosity and had no intention of turning them over to the authorities.

Ruby and I made a quick assessment of the situation. The upper deck of the smugglers' boat was dark, an indication that they did not plan to move tonight. The crew was apparently sleeping, maybe dreaming of the profits from their next trip. The distance from their mooring point to the landing bay was over four kilometers (two and a half miles), so even if our activity was noticed, they were too far away to interfere. All that had to be done was to mark an alternative route westward for the big Zodiacs bypassing the smugglers' craft.

What we had to do now was to check the landing beach, which was surrounded by hills, and make sure that no surprises awaited us there.

Moving slowly, we arrived at "Fridge Bay" — thus called because of the rusty metal shell of what had once been a refrigerator, which had reached its shore under unclear circumstances.

The bay was relatively wide, free of coral reefs and had a sandy bottom sloping gently toward the water. An added advantage was easy access from the main north-south traffic artery. The hills surrounding it concealed it from the travelers on the main axis. Incidentally, that "central north-south traffic artery" was nothing but a sandy path traveled during the day by a few dozen trucks. At night, the axis was completely deserted, except for some very rare military and police patrols hunting — usually unsuccessfully — for smuggler convoys.

We entered the bay slowly. The Zodiac's 40 hp motor worked at the lowest rpm's endowed it by the manufacturer, so as not to leave a blazing trail of lights in the water caused by the blending of shiny microscopic sea organisms. Israeli naval commandos call the trails "*hass-pen-tai'rs* (hush lest you wake it)," taken from a well-known poem by the national Israeli poet Haim Nahman Bialik, "A Bird's Nest," which contains the line "three eggs, inside each — hush lest you wake it — a tiny chick sleeps."

Ruby navigated toward the "Fridge" shore, and I stood on the bow observing it with binoculars. Dead silence. Nothing was moving.

Twenty meters away from the shore, I got off the boat, armed with binoculars and a two-way radio. The cold water reached my navel. I moved slowly with a racing heart.

Another ten meters, five meters more. I got out of the water, slumped behind an earth mound and scanned the area with my binoculars. All of a sudden a brown mass jumped in front of my eyes, letting out a jarring squeal.

I have had many adventures during my service with the Mossad, but the only time I recall being on the verge of cardiac arrest was that night behind the earth mound on the shore of "Fridge Bay" in Sudan. That brown mass was none other than a poor, scared fox.

"All's well?" asked Ruby on the radio.

"Yes," I answered after I managed to calm down a bit. "I'm climbing to the top to take a look at the area."

Ruby waited in the boat, and I climbed onto the earth and rock mound overlooking the bay, about two hundred meters from the shore. I scanned the area with my binoculars. Still quiet. Nothing was moving.

"Okay," I reported to Ruby. "Everything's quiet, go in peace."

Ruby copied and in low gear motored toward the outer reefs to await the arrival of the naval boats.

Chapter 29

The quiet around me was overwhelming. I couldn't but reflect how fate moves in weird ways. Only several months earlier I quit the Mossad to protest its intervention in my private affairs, and here I was, sitting alone on a desolate hill in the heart of the Sudanese desert, thousands of kilometers from Tel Aviv…and no one was interfering with my life.

I tried to picture the state of tension right then at the Mossad operations control, at the height of monitoring the deployment of forces: the *INS Bat Galim* — at sea; the naval commando Zodiacs already within Sudanese territorial waters, moving toward a rendezvous with Ruby; our vehicles, led by Danny, traveling in a convoy moving slowly along the dirt tracks bypassing Port Sudan, laden with more than 170 fatigued and starved Jewish refugees. And here I was stuck on a barren mound in the heart of the Sudanese desert, armed with binoculars, a two-way radio and a bar of chocolate.

From my right came the distant call of a desert animal, perhaps a camel. From my vantage point I observed the sandy track that our convoy was supposed to emerge from. Absolute silence.

The radio was still emitting only static. I arranged myself a seat among the rocks. I broke up the chocolate bar into squares to pass the time and also to consume them slowly so as to remain alert longer.

Time crawled. All of a sudden my little two-way radio woke up: "Danny here. Can you read me? We'll be with you in an hour. What's the situation?"

Short messages replaced the static. Coordination of the meet between Ruby and the naval boats. A short report from Danny for the benefit of the front command honchos on the *Bat Galim* vessel.

The fatigue disappeared completely. The adrenalin started flowing.

Minutes later, our convoy reached the shore.

"Stay in the lookout position. Let me know what happens," Danny told me on the radio. He sounded extremely tense, unlike his usual self. I trained my binoculars on the beach. Danny, Dr. Pomeranz, Eli, Shmulik and Joe began unloading the "brothers" from the vehicles and grouping them in preparation for boarding.

Some of them went to the edge of the water and tried to quench their thirst. They did not expect the salty taste, since for most or even all of them this was their first encounter with the beach and the sea.

There was no order there. I saw people searching for their bundles of belongings on the trucks. Mothers were searching for their children. I heard babies crying. They moved to the side of the pathway in small groups to urinate.

From afar came the hum of motors of the naval boats following Ruby's little Zodiac into the bay.

I was scanning the hills around us. Suddenly my binoculars caught a suspicious movement on the range that bounded the bay to the west. I focused my binoculars. No doubt. People were moving on the ridge several hundred meters opposite me. "We have guests," I radioed Danny quietly. "I see movement on the ridge across from me."

"Follow them and let me know what's happening," Danny said in a strained voice. From the beach wafted exhortations to speed up. I no longer needed binoculars to see the silhouettes of the Zodiacs jockeying along the beaching line, the navy term for the point where they go ashore. Suddenly the moon shone, painting the bay with a strip of light, making the silhouettes stand out even more.

It would have been an exceptionally romantic tableau, were it not for the unidentified images within range. I scanned the area across the horizon. Now I could see several shadows moving in the small wadi at the foot of the hill where I lay. I had no doubt that the unknowns could not see me. I was hidden among the rocks, under the skyline, wearing a dark scuba suit.

"There is traffic around me like in Trafalgar Square," I calmly reported to Danny. "These may be Bedouins, perhaps smugglers whose work we interrupted, or even worse." Danny copied my report. "Let me know if they start moving toward the beach, that is, in our direction."

I heard Danny tell Ruby and the officer commanding the naval boats to beach all the boats and then start moving the "brothers" out to deep water.

The large rubber dinghies hit the sandy beach like whales having lost their sense of direction. Aided by members of our team, the "brothers" were taken to the boats and sat down per instructions, on the wooden bottom in the center.

"A group of people is moving slowly from the ridge in your direction. At the foot of the hill to the left of my position there are a few more people observing you," I reported to Danny.

It was clear to all of us that something had gone very wrong.

"Get off the hill and join us. Hurry," he said.

I gladly abandoned the nameless hill I had occupied for several hours of my life. Within a minute, I was down on the beach with the rest of the team.

"I don't know who they are, but I want us to evacuate the beach, urgently," Danny told Gadi Kroll, commander of the naval commando force. "Load up and put to sea. No waiting. Each boat that fills up must leave the shore immediately and wait out at sea. On the double!" Danny ordered in a calm edging on hysteria.

Within a few seconds all the Zodiacs were in the water, slowly moving in circles to await the last boat, which had gotten stuck on the beach, heavily laden with frightened "brothers."

I ran toward the boat. Shmulik and two young commandos tried to push it into the water. I went to help them. The boat wouldn't budge.

"*Irfau idcum* (hands up)!" came a loud shout in Arabic from the direction of a group of soldiers that was moving quickly toward us from the western range. Even though they were far away from us, we could see that they were armed.

On the beach remained the stranded boat with scores of "brothers," two soldiers, a Toyota pickup truck, a small International truck packed with gear and threadbare packages belonging to "brothers," and Mossad agents Danny, Eli, Joe, Dr. Shlomo Pomeranz, Shmulik and myself.

No one raised their hands, of course. Shmulik expertly pulled out his commando knife, but at the sight of the Kalashnikovs held by the approaching soldiers, quickly sheathed it.

We kept up our frantic efforts to extricate the stranded boat. Danny, known for courage bordering on insanity, sought to gain time and shouted something like "Wait a minute" toward the officer who led the soldiers. We noticed the sparks emitted from the muzzle of the Kalashnikov at the same time we heard the firing. One of the Sudanese soldiers, or perhaps the officer himself, tried to use this to speed up the decision-making process of those facing him and convince them to raise their hands.

Tabloids and television shows love to air testimonials of people who at a certain moment, under threat to their lives, manage to summon superhuman powers, like the father who lifted half a truck to pull out his son who had been crushed under its wheels. This is precisely what happened to the two naval commandos and Shmulik and me, while extricating the stubborn boat. Suddenly it yielded to our combined effort as if it were stuck in a mound of butter, not sand, and slid across the sand and into the Red Sea waters.

All this took only several seconds. In the meantime Sudanese soldiers reached Danny and his crew, about fifty meters behind us, making encouraging shouts in the face of an event that was totally foreign to them, while Danny and his men raised their hands. Some of the Sudanese soldiers started running toward our boat, which floated leisurely in the shallow water, a meter or two away from the shoreline. Shmulik and the two commandos quickly boarded the boat. I remained in the water, one arm clutching the two-way radio up high to keep it from getting wet, and the other pushing the boat into deeper water.

One of the soldiers tried to start the motor with quick, deft movements. But like in the movies, as if to increase the tension, the motor refused to give in at this critical moment. From the corner of my eye I could see that Shmulik had already pulled out his knife. To be on the safe side.

"Take out your weapons!" I shouted at our soldiers.

"You won't believe it, but the weapons are stuck under the feet of dozens of passengers," one of them replied softly. The passengers, some twenty Jews of all ages, sat huddled together, scared, not understanding what was going on around them.

On the third try, the motor went into action. The Zodiac moved heavily toward the center of the bay, laden to the rim. Shmulik extended his hand and helped me aboard.

"Stop, don't go on," I told the SEAL who was driving the boat. "We must wait to see what is happening."

"We're the last boat, and only we can report the event," Shmulik explained to the SEALs.

Several hundred meters behind us came the roar of motors from the Zodiacs that had managed to escape before the incident. No doubt they had heard the shots, but didn't know where they originated.

The entire incident, from the moment the shout "raise your hands" was heard to the firing of the volley in our direction and our moving away from the beach, lasted maybe a minute. A very long minute.

From about one hundred meters away, we witnessed a surrealistic scene on the shore. The moon, its rays intensified by its reflection in the quiet bay water, lit the whole area with a bright light. On the beach stood Danny, Eli, Dr. Pomeranz and Joe, their hands raised, facing cocked Kalashnikovs with the safety off.

Sometime later, Danny recounted that at the critical moment, when it appeared that they would be cut down by assault rifle fire at close range, Dr. Pomeranz whispered crazily to him in Hebrew á la Mel Brooks, "What say, Boss, shouldn't we waste them?" thus lending greater credence to Hassan's diagnosis of "nutcases."

From our Zodiac, the scene now seemed like one taken from a war film, where Gestapo men ring a bunch of courageous underground fighters.

"Attention all stations," I radioed in an excited tone, in English of course. "All the 'brothers' were pulled out safely. But four of our men are stranded on the beach surrounded by armed hostile elements. We must quickly put together a rescue force before they are taken prisoner."

Ruby, who was already deep into the bay with the rest of the Navy SEAL force under Gadi Kroll's command, copied my message. Kroll's men recounted later that the moment the shots were heard his nostrils flared. "I can smell gunpowder," he said, huffing and puffing like a veteran battle horse. "Come on, boys, get your weapons out!"

It was clear to anyone there that this incident marked the end of the operation to extricate the Jews from the refugee camps in Sudan. The commander of the operation and three of his men had been caught red-handed in a Sudanese army ambush. Left on the ground were countless indications of extraordinary activity going on only a few minutes earlier. Clear drag marks in the sand, a truck laden with packages and refugees' bundles of clothing. And if this was not enough, the same Sudanese soldiers I had identified earlier on the ridge opposite us, and reported to Danny, had watched how empty boats came ashore, and many people getting off vehicles boarded them and sailed out to sea.

Why and how did the soldiers reach this site on that particular evening? The answer came retroactively in debriefing and postmortem sessions. These suggested that the Sudanese were dispatched to the area to set an ambush for smugglers who were intensifying their activity at the time. The data pointed to the possibility that the patrol spotted our small convoy under Danny's command as it made its way northward from Port Sudan, including the red truck which was adapted to local conditions, just like a convoy of smugglers.

Sudanese soldiers, moving in two large jeeps with headlights switched off, monitored our convoy from afar without being noticed, right up to the "Fridge Bay." From the western range they watched the weird activity taking place on the beach.

Why didn't they interfere at an earlier stage? We can only surmise that the officer leading the Sudanese force was concerned that the unknowns he was watching were heavily armed. Therefore, he waited until nearly all of them had left the beach except for the last members of the group, and the single boat that got stuck on the sand, and then ordered his men to move.

But Danny, thrust unwittingly into this incident, showed rare courage and resourcefulness, yet again managing to get out of the tight spot he found himself in. His hands raised above his head, facing excited Sudanese soldiers poking the barrels of their Kalashnikovs in his stomach, he didn't lose his wits, but rather assumed control. Suddenly he started screaming at the Sudanese officer at the top of his voice. "What are you doing, you fool?" he shouted. "Are you out of your mind, shooting at tourists?"

The officer, who understood English, was stunned. His soldiers stood petrified by the shouting. Danny's team members stared at him with admiration.

Encouraged by his gambit, Danny put down his arms and continued to exploit his initial advantage. "I'm going to complain about you to the chief of staff," he screamed, flailing his arms menacingly. "Can't you see that we are organizing night diving here for tourists? We work for the Tourism Ministry, bringing tourists from all over the world to acquaint them with the beauty of Sudan, and all you fools can do is fire at us! Just like that, without warning! You must be out of your mind!"

The officer began muttering something, and Danny took up the shouting tactic again, raising his voice an octave or two. "Who's the idiot that made you an officer? Can't you see what you're doing?"

"I'm sorry," the officer stuttered. "I didn't know those were tourists; I thought you were smugglers."

At this point, I must say a few words in praise of the surprising retreat of that junior officer, leading a miserable unit of Sudanese soldiers, whose sole task was to lie in wait for smugglers. No one seemed to have prepared him for the possibility of encountering a bunch of Europeans on a godforsaken bay engaged in mysterious and strange activity, the likes of which he had never seen.

It's impossible to know what went through his mind during those long moments when he surreptitiously watched our people in action, with no way of understanding what was going on. No sheep were being smuggled, nor consumer goods, and certainly no weapons either. All he saw was dozens of men, women and children boarding large boats and sailing out to sea.

Was he thinking of the explanation he had to provide to his commanders about the night's events? In addition, to compound his problems, he was confronted by a *hawaja* (foreign master) fuming with anger who mentioned the army chief of staff as though he were a family member and threatened to ruin his career.

The messages coming out of the two-way radio indicated to Danny that in a few moments a naval commando rescue team was about to descend on the beach to prevent him and his men from being captured by the evil Sudanese.

"Attention," Danny's voice was heard on the radio, a bit excited but perfectly clear. "We are absolutely well. Repeat: everything's under control. Don't come back ashore. I repeat again: do not return to the beach. Carry on according to plans. We shall meet later in the village."

I could see Danny well from my vantage point atop the bow of the Zodiac. What helped was the small distance between us and the beach. We could see clearly that he was radioing of his own free will and that no Kalashnikov barrel was pointed at his head. At that stage, apparently on orders of the confused and embarrassed officer, the soldiers stopped threatening Danny and his men. They broke the circle that ringed the four white men, and some of them started checking the contents of the truck and the bundles left behind on the beach by the "brothers."

European soldiers would have noted easily that someone was trying to dupe them, if only because of the bundles, which clearly didn't belong to tourists. But the strange story concocted instantly by Danny about a group of tourists out for a nighttime tour along the Red Sea appeared plausible to the adversary — a Sudanese soldier who had never seen a European vacation site — despite the suspicious tattered bundles on the truck. The basic rule of illegal covert activity, that the situation must be evaluated by taking the adversary's thinking into consideration, proved itself yet again.

To be on the safe side, Danny repeated his message a third time. "There was a misunderstanding. It is being clarified as we speak. We shall meet later in the village."

We remained a few moments longer at our vantage point opposite the beach to make sure that everything was going well. Danny's words were clear and unequivocal, but in light of the sharp fluctuations in the situation over the last few moments, like a fiendishly steep rollercoaster for people with particularly strong hearts, we were still under a cloud of confusion and uncertainty. Through the binoculars I could see that Danny was still talking with the officer, but now without shouting and hand-waving. Dr. Pomeranz and Joe were moving freely on the beach, gathering equipment and putting it on the truck. The soldiers stared at them and the vehicles and watched the conversation between Danny and their officer. Some of them were smoking.

"Move on. We're joining the rest of the force," I told the SEALs, and within minutes we linked up with the long convoy of boats along the route Ruby and I mapped out at the start of the evening. Now, by the moonlight, we noticed the silhouette of the smuggler boat at the far end of the *marsa*. Not a single ray of light came out of it.

If they had heard the shots, they decided to play dead and appear to be sleeping.

Next to the marker where the incident with the osprey occurred, we took leave of the naval commandos and moved into our small Zodiac craft. The naval boats set out on a long voyage of more than an hour's high-speed cruising in the open sea, the destination being the *Bat Galim*, which was waiting outside Sudan's territorial waters.

The quick trip back to shore was spent analyzing the situation. It was clear to us that the short-term danger was over, and we estimated that we would be evacuated from Sudan that night.

On reaching the village we tied the Zodiac to the makeshift pier and began preparing for a possible evacuation. We readied another boat and filled up the reserve fuel tanks. Afterward, we went to the boat equipment shed and rounded up everything we thought should not be left behind, from communications gear to particularly expensive spare parts. Only then did we go to our rooms and each of us prepared an emergency bundle complete with clothes, money and passports.

Chapter 30

Our local workers were sleeping or pretended that they were. We went back to the pier to wait for Danny and the rest of the group. We agreed that should a car be seen approaching the village, we would move into the boats, so that if it turned out that the arrivals were policemen or soldiers, we could release the moorings and flee by sea.

Our walkie-talkies were good only over a very short range. We could pick up short-range traffic but the rest came in truncated. We understood that the naval commando boats had not yet linked up with the mother vessel, and that in the meantime urgent consultations were going on with Danny regarding the next moves. We were relieved. The meaning of this was that Danny had managed to clear up the misunderstanding with the officer and was now free as a bird.

I remember that despite the nerve-racking wait, it was impossible not to enjoy the amazing scene. A sliver of the moon painted the edge of the lagoon with a strip of silver, and the movement of the schools of fish caused the surface to break into myriad sparks of light. The sky was studded with bright stars, and tiny waves lapped the beach silently.

I no longer remember how long it took for Danny and his bunch to join us. Danny was standing on the roof of the Toyota attempting to increase the range of his radio and continuing to discuss the next moves.

"There were very unpleasant moments there," Dr. Pomeranz was reconstructing the tense moments on the beach. "We were sure they were going to take the boat as well, but then you managed to extricate yourselves at the last moment. What luck. The Sudanese were nervous as cats and as a seasoned paratrooper I was appalled to notice that their Kalashnikovs were cocked with the safeties set to 'Automatic.' What a scary situation." Still this had not kept him from joking nonchalantly with Danny!

Apke, the oldest member of the bunch, was pale. Small wonder. He, who survived the Holocaust as a boy, never imagined that his readiness to go to Sudan to help with the logistics of the rescue of Ethiopian Jews would end up with him staring at the wrong end of a Sudanese Kalashnikov.

Joe, who so far had restricted his daily smoking to three Gitane cigarettes after meals, was now chain-smoking.

We talked quietly in Hebrew, knowing that the noise of the sea muffled our voices and that if one of our Sudanese workers was observing us, he would hear nothing.

Our mood shifted from one extreme to the other. A clear-headed appraisal of the conditions on the ground indicated that the only sane option was to abandon everything, start up the boats and link up with the *Bat Galim*. No doubt, if it were purely an intelligence mission, Mossad headquarters wouldn't have hesitated for a moment to instruct us to sail east to the boat, and then home, to a heroes' welcome befitting men who persevered in their mission in an enemy country to the last minute, and under fire too.

But this was not an intelligence mission. Our mission in Sudan was one of the sort that made Mossad, the Institute for Intelligence and Special Operations, a legend in the spy world. What other developed country would be ready to invest tens of millions of dollars to set up an operational infrastructure for secret activity in an enemy country, involving large army forces, only to save several thousand famished refugees in civil war-torn Africa? The most that the enlightened world would have considered doing for these refugees was raising money in donations, sometimes by holding mass rock concerts, and disbursing sums of charity money, certainly small compared with the huge budgets for armaments that characterized the height of the Cold War era.

The human aspect of this operation made us ponder the full repercussions of abandoning Sudan. What would befall the other "brothers" if indeed we were ordered out? How could we leave them behind in the unbearable conditions they endured? Soon we came to think of it as abandoning comrades in the battlefield, or even betrayal!

We knew that someone in the Sudanese leadership, perhaps Nimeiri himself, was aware that Jewish refugees were leaving Sudan by way of Khartoum in a thin trickle, under the cover of a foreign aid agency. But the entire military aspect of the rescue operations was conducted clandestinely, and in case of a leak, all of us were certain candidates for grueling and humiliating interrogations with all that they entailed. After several hours of consultations, discussions, exchanges of views and whatnot, the decision was made.

We remain in Sudan.

But it was clear to all that following the incident in "Fridge Bay" the situation had changed radically. The maritime route had exhausted itself.

Mossad headquarters swiftly came to the conclusion that there was no choice but to change the operations method in order to reduce the risks. Gathering the "brothers" at a rendezvous point close to the camp was and would remain the Achilles heel of the entire operation. Headquarters were racking their brains to find a way to avoid the long and perilous rides of trucks heavily packed with refugees. Shorter trips would mean running fewer roadblocks, whether by force or guile, greatly reducing the risk of mishaps that could lead to disaster.

Another option had been discussed at headquarters in the past: an airlift. Merely six years earlier, Israeli Air Force transport aircraft had proved that operating in the heart of the African continent was not a matter of fantasy. The distance between Israel and Sudan as the crow flies is shorter than the distance between Israel and Entebbe, Uganda.

And now that the maritime rescue route had fallen through, at least for now, it was time for the air force to get into the picture.

But the shift to aerial operations required many preparations and in the meantime we abandoned the village, temporarily of course, and returned to Israel via Europe to recharge our energies and organize for the new phase of operations.

Our loyal workers, who remained in the village and didn't understand why not a single tourist had arrived, were told that we were going to Europe to pull together everything necessary for the Arous Holiday Village to get on the international tourism map.

Our return to civilization wasn't abrupt. Ruby and I had a gradual homecoming from the village to Port Sudan, then to the Khartoum Hilton, and on to Europe aboard a foreign airline. Standing orders were that not even in an emergency could one board a long-range flight of "Inshallah Airways."

And thus, nearly three months after leaving the Holy Land, Ruby and I came back on a short home leave. Awaiting us at the arrivals hall of Ben-Gurion Airport was Ephraim with the heroic greeting from Menachem Begin, the prime minister.

Chapter 31

The cool breeze blowing atop one of the Erkowit range ridges made us forget for a little while that we were in Sudan. To anyone who came here from the burning furnace of the coastal plain, which averaged 35 degrees (95 Fahrenheit) and unbearable humidity, the clear Erkowit air had a luxurious quality, something that to an average Tel Avivian would be reminiscent of the "clear as a claret mountain air" of Jerusalem.

But Tel Aviv was far away. Our short home leave, just over a month, had been forgotten. The question "where did you disappear to?" put by family members and friends produced a mumbled reply about some work assignment in Europe. Above all, I found it difficult to explain to my eldest son, who was six years old at the time. I may have been a great patriot then, but certainly did not deserve the "Father of the Year" award. Shortly afterward I disappeared again, for another three long months.

In the midst of the vacation we were summoned to attend a detailed postmortem of all the events of "the night of the shooting at 'Fridge Bay.'" Everyone reconstructed that night's events, which luckily ended peacefully — without captives, injuries and evidently without significant damage to the operation. After further deliberations, based on this updated input, it was finally decided that it was possible to continue our operation in Sudan.

Truth be told, home leave was interrupted every few days because of something linked in some way to the Sudan operation. I was sent, for instance, to attend a brush-up session, improvised at that, on "checking the features of a landing strip." In a small office at air force headquarters, a young officer took a certain device out of a cabinet, which was supposed to help us in the field.

The actual practice with the device took exactly two minutes. I put the device together under the watchful eyes of the officer, who didn't stop rushing me, because it was almost midday by the clock, and that day chicken breast schnitzel was served in the mess hall. "And I love schnitzel," he added.

"May luck be with you," the officer summed up the practice session. He made me sign an ordnance slip, handed me the miracle gadget and disappeared along the pathway of the Kiryah, the defense ministry complex in Tel Aviv, toward the mess hall and the promised schnitzel.

Our brief home visit was also used to practice procedures for landing C-130 Hercules transports. Sounds simple, but it nevertheless requires teamwork and a lot of practice, since any mistake, thousands of miles away in Sudan, could have serious repercussions. "Remember the blooper the Americans had when they tried to release their hostages from the embassy in Tehran," the instructors said. "Get into your heads the images of the burned-out Hercules transports and helicopter skeletons at the center of the makeshift landing site in the desert, not to mention the political implications of such a failure. You can ask Jimmy Carter, who a short time later was forced to leave his cozy office in the White House adorned with a loser's halo."

It stood to reason that the person who decided to dispatch military aircraft to Sudan took into consideration the worst-case scenario: a packed news conference in Khartoum, for instance, where an Israeli Air Force crew and a paratroop platoon sent to secure the landing site would be paraded like monkeys in a traveling circus. "An example of the expansionist aspirations of Zionist imperialism," someone would say, and the cameras would record the torn uniforms and the faded look in the prisoners' eyes. And this was an optimistic scenario compared to a possible press tour, led by the Sudanese information minister, to some remote spot in the desert, where he would be photographed against the backdrop of a burned-out aircraft skeleton and charred bodies, pointing to a small Star of David on the tail section of the crashed Hercules.

But we decided to leave the agonizing and the decisions to the pencil pushers at Mossad headquarters. We focused on practical aspects of the operation. Our job was to mark out the landing strip for the approaching aircraft. After landing, we were to deploy the soldiers of the security unit around the site, make sure that no one was left on the ground, and enable the aircraft to take off to its destination.

Unlike the maritime operations, where the presence of IDF forces on Sudanese soil was limited to a few moments on the far fringes of the country, this involved a blatant penetration of Sudanese air space, followed by landing of enemy forces in the heart of the country. The role of the soldiers there was to secure us, because we were unarmed. In the event that uninvited visitors, such as a small group of policemen, would show up, the soldiers would take care of them, but nothing beyond that.

No one wanted to run battles on Sudanese soil. Several Kalashnikov bullets hitting the aircraft could be catastrophic. Therefore we were ordered to confirm beyond a shadow of doubt that the area was free of military or police patrols prior to the aircraft landing. Dry runs were carried out in northern Israel. After several exercises we achieved a performance level that satisfied the Hercules pilots, air force representatives and chief paratroop officer Brigadier General Amos Yaron, whose troops were used as the security force to the operation and because of that, closely monitored the joint exercises.

Thus in early May Ruby and I returned to Sudan, which was in the midst of summer, as an advance force ahead of the resumption of the operation to rescue the Ethiopian Jews from Sudan.

Our baggage included all sorts of gear. I no longer remember what cover story we made up that time, but since our loyal representative, who waited for us at Khartoum Airport, lavished a reasonable sum of money on anyone he considered useful for the cause, no one even bothered to open our cases.

The next few days saw the arrival of the rest of the crew, headed by Danny. We all gathered again in the Khartoum Hilton ahead of resumption of operations.

This time the team was bolstered by new faces. For instance, there was Louis, an amiable and energetic young man with a crazy sense of humor who was an alumnus of the Navy SEALs, and Gil, a mechanic who could breathe life into a dead chunk of metal — for example a very old generator in a forgotten spot in Sudan that had not been serviced or maintained for the last ten years.

That evening was the eve of Israeli Independence Day, and on this holiday, we were told, it was permissible for a Mossad man staying in an enemy country to step into the most expensive restaurant in town, order a wickedly expensive meal and raise a silent toast.

We did that in the Ivory Club, the prestigious Hilton Hotel restaurant. The darkened and elegant restaurant was blessed with a rich wine cellar, all the more distinctive because of its geographical location. The maitre d' was an intelligent fellow from Chad, who spoke superb French and English. He was happy to decant for the merry band of men the best of French vintage wines, which had found their way intact to Khartoum, two bottles per course.

I only remember that the food was excellent, and the main course an ultra-soft fillet steak. The restaurant was empty, except for one table on the fringe of the darkened hall, where a man was sitting alone facing a bottle of wine, staring at us with envy. Yes, he too was on the Mossad payroll, the replacement for our friend Uri, whom we had met in the government guesthouse in Gedaref. Following the rules of covert activity, and particularly compartmentalization of operations, we ignored his presence.

As the alcohol level in our blood went up, we were overcome with silliness. We drank toasts in foreign languages, and toward the end of the meal I decided that a sing-along would be an appropriate way to round off the event. I started singing "All the Country, Flags and Flags," a popular Hebrew Independence Day song, and having discovered that the simultaneous translation into English was working, I went on with "Oh ho the Foxes of Samson." Those sitting around the table joined my quiet singing. "These are Irish and Scottish folk songs," we told the Chadian maitre d', who that evening earned the tip of a lifetime. We ended with a well-known popular tune, "To the Garden of Nuts I Descended," the last note of which prompted the lonely man sitting across from us to point a finger to his temple in a circular motion. "You are nuts," he indicated, but couldn't suppress the broad smile on his face.

The next day, suffering from huge hangovers, but with joy in our hearts, we embarked on the long road back to the village to get organized for the aerial operation.

That week Danny and I had already been to the Erkowit range, less than two hundred kilometers (125 miles) from our village, taking in the magnificent view and looking for an appropriate patch of territory to land transport aircraft.

From our vantage point, on the hood of the Toyota, we followed dozens of huge eagles circling lazily while utilizing the columns of warm air that rose from the coastal plain.

The balmy weather and the wild mountainous scenery beneath us, so different from that of the level steppes of the Nile Delta, convinced Sudan's colonial rulers to set up a small holiday village at this particular spot. This included a row of low-slung stone structures, a lone tennis court and a clubhouse with a wide terrace overlooking the scenery, where generations of colonial officials probably sat watching the sun set with whiskey glasses in their hands. It was the traditional "Sundowner" ritual observed by Her Majesty's emissaries across the Empire, which spread from one end of the world to the other and on which the sun never set.

The British remained in Sudan for sixty years. Attesting to the significance of this huge country to the builders of the Empire was the Fashoda Incident, which more than a hundred years ago threatened to throw Britain and France into total war. At the end of the nineteenth century, Britain, France and Germany were involved in a race for control of homesteads in Africa. The battle for the Nile and its sources was particularly acute.

Attempting to create facts on the ground, a small French military contingent left Chad in the summer of 1896 and headed eastward, led by a courageous officer named Marchand. In Africa of the late nineteenth century, movement from place to place was by sailing along rivers or by slow marching on foot. Attempts to import horses to speed up the pace of movement failed due to lethal attacks of tsetse flies.

After two years of trouble, sickness and clashes with local tribes that had no interest in unilateral association with the French Empire, Marchand's group reached the small town of Fashoda on the bank of the Nile. On July 10, 1898, Marchand raised the tricolor in a small ceremony, claiming all of southern Sudan for France.

Weeks later, reports reached Paris about the modest ceremony in Fashoda, making every French citizen proud. France's colonial dream of taking control of all of central Africa, from the shores of the Atlantic Ocean to the Nile, was about to be realized. In addition, a mixed French-Ethiopian unit took up positions on the other bank of the Nile, after a backbreaking march from Ethiopia. Unlike Paris, London responded to the news about Marchand's move with fury. The architects of the British Empire had aspired to set up a contiguous chain of British territories from the Cape of Good Hope to Cairo and dreamed of a railway that would connect the two places. Marchand's small tricolor, fluttering with Gaelic insolence from an improvised pole in faraway Fashoda, was a potential threat to that contiguity.

Official British policy held categorically that the French had no business on the Nile and should the French fail to understand that, it was said in London, the policy would be made clear to them by force, including full-scale war if necessary. The British threat to remove Marchand was not an idle one. Unlike France, the British had a huge army in Sudan — an expeditionary force under the command of General Kitchener, which in those very days was about to conclude a tough and notably costly battle to sweep the Mahdi and his supporters out of Khartoum and the Nile Valley.

A few years earlier, the Mahdi mercilessly drove out the Egyptians and the Turks who ruled Sudan, took Khartoum, murdered thousands of Egyptians and Sudanese who worked for the hated Egyptian rulers and cut Sudan off from the rest of the world.

The Mahdi reached the headlines in the contemporary European press, because during the time of the conquest of Khartoum from the Egyptian garrison, his frenzied soldiers killed the much admired British commander General Charles Gordon. Thus, Kitchener's expeditionary force was ready to carry out additional assignments, considered essential for expanding the British Empire.

Another attempt by the British Foreign Office to force the French government to order Marchand out of Fashoda failed immediately and London decided that talk was not enough. Thus, minutes after Kitchener routed the Mahdi army in the Battle of Omdurman, he rushed to Fashoda at the head of a large force, and stood at its gates in September of 1898.

Although Marchand's small unit, which had lost its supply line two years earlier, stood no chance against Kitchener's regular troops, the Frenchman spurned Kitchener's ultimatum.

Faced with Marchand's arrogant rejection, Kitchener dropped the diplomatic lingo, and switched to a blunt style of speech.

"Get out!" Kitchener ordered.

"Only after Britain recognizes our claim to the region," Marchand replied with emphasis, acting on orders he had received on the eve of his mission two years earlier.

"That's out of the question," said Kitchener.

"I'm not leaving here, unless I receive an explicit order from my government," Marchand insisted. It must be said to Kitchener's credit that although he was aware of the French limitations, and even though it was patently clear that Marchand had no chance against him militarily, Kitchener allowed him to contact Paris for fresh instructions.

Fashoda was then one of the remotest places in the world. But seeing the noisy headlines in the European press, readers could easily believe that it was a bustling key town and that anyone controlling it could view half of Africa as his.

Not to be outdone, the French news correspondents described in the minutest detail, largely invented, the stubborn stand of Captain Marchand in faraway Fashoda. Those descriptions contained all the ingredients necessary to fan patriotism among the French public, and particularly in the summer and fall of 1898.

Because of the Dreyfus Affair, French society was divided into two camps. In August of that year, 1898, it had been revealed that Colonel Henri, head of military intelligence, forged the documents that led to the conviction of the Jewish officer Alfred Dreyfus for treason. The army chief, General Boisdeffre, resigned. Colonel Henri was arrested and committed suicide. Dreyfus's wife demanded a retrial. The reports about Marchand's brave and stubborn stand in Fashoda in the face of the thieving British landed in the midst of this melee, giving fresh ammunition to the depleted armories of French patriots.

"Don't give in. Fashoda is ours, and so is the Nile," shouted multitudes in Paris. "War! We want war!"

In Britain too, there were protests, and diplomats on both sides began looking for allies. The British signed a secret pact with Germany and the French signed up with the Russians, and indeed both began preparations for war.

Excitement ran high in Europe for a few more weeks. In Fashoda, however, both sides maintained restraint; perhaps due to the geographic distance from home, which caused the officers on the ground to remain level-headed.

The war hysteria, mainly in France, continued. Historians emphasize that never since 1815 had France and Britain been as close to war as during the Fashoda crisis.

Pouring cold water onto the war-frenzy were the French admirals, who made it clear to the government in plain language that in case of a war, which would necessarily also be a naval war, the French navy stood no chance against the British might.

Following heated debates in the cabinet, including accusations of treason and cowardice, the French government was forced to give in. It took a few days for the evacuation order to reach Marchand, and only in November did Marchand read the orders to lower the tricolor in Fashoda and retreat westward. The boundary between the British and French territories was established hundreds of kilometers west of the Nile and thus Sudan remained under Egyptian-British control until 1956. The recreation site of choice for British officials who sweated, came down with Malaria and other exotic diseases, and developed Sudan whilst simultaneously exploiting its riches, was the modest camp at Erkowit. There, Danny and I arrived in the Sudanese summer of 1982 to break ground for the incorporation of air force planes in the operation to rescue Ethiopian Jews from Sudan.

Chapter 32

The request from headquarters was short and clear: "We need information about possible landing sites south of Port Sudan."

Technically, the Hercules transports had the capacity to reach Sudan, but this required installing extra fuel tanks and an exact plotting of the flight route. True, the Israeli Air Force flew farther to reach Entebbe, Uganda, in 1976, but then they had a refueling stop in Nairobi.

There had almost been air force involvement in the second naval operation we ran. During that operation a young girl with high fever was brought onto the *Bat Galim*. The doctors promptly diagnosed an acute case of meningitis. Her condition was deteriorating rapidly and lacking proper support equipment aboard, her life was seriously threatened.

Speed was never one of the attributes of the *INS Bat Galim*, and therefore a request went out to the air force command to put a Sikorsky CH-53 helicopter on standby to pick up the girl at sea, off Sudanese shores. Because of the distance from Israel, such a maneuver required meticulous planning, including numerous midair refuelings of the chopper. But after a quick check, air force operations announced: "No problem, we're ready."

No one questioned the need to scramble a helicopter or the refueling aircraft for a risky operation, far from home base, to save the life of a girl who had not even received an Israeli ID.

During the night, her condition improved and the helicopter rescue was called off. Immediately afterward, headquarters sent us, in a circuitous way, a small shipment of meningitis vaccines.

Despite Sudan's membership in the Arab League, and the fact that it had sent token units to fight against us in the Independence,

Six-Day and Yom Kippur Wars, it wasn't considered an enemy country in direct conflict with Israel. Therefore, the air force probably had incomplete data about the country, based mostly on aerial photos and obsolete maps. Thus we were charged with gathering data on the ground to assist with the planning of the aerial rescue.

As part of this effort, Marcel and I had left several days earlier for a long tour of the Gedaref region. We covered a territory the size of Israel's northern Galilee region. It was densely populated, relative to Sudanese standards of course, and had dozens of refugee camps. We were on the lookout for a barren patch of land, away from civilization, which did not have even one shepherd's shed, since an aircraft landing at night sends out ripples of sound that can be heard from afar and was bound to bring undesirable onlookers to the landing site. As we went further south, the refugee camps disappeared. In their place were corn and sorghum fields, stretching across the horizon. I had never seen such tall corn plants.

Well-packed paths crisscrossed the corn fields, part of an ambitious project of Arab oil-exporting countries to turn Sudan into a grain storehouse for the Muslim world. The project was born after the Yom Kippur War, when the oil countries' coffers swelled with petrodollars.

The vast corn fields of Gedaref were another example of Sudan's chronic ills, and of its failure to use the crops to feed the poor and famished people of Africa. At a huge financial investment, the land was cultivated. Seeds were sown. Every few kilometers a regional service station was erected, containing housing quarters for workers and machinery sheds. The beginning was promising. But after two or three seasons, difficulties arose. Due to the lack of a pool of experienced technicians and mechanics, any minor breakdown or absence of a small screw worth only a few cents would cripple tens of thousands of dollars worth of sophisticated equipment. One after another, the sophisticated harvesters, Canadian made I believe, went out of commission. The crop they harvested usually did not reach the consumers, whether for lack of trucks or because the silos housed hordes of mice and rats that feasted on the abundant petrodollar-grown corn.

Our tour of Gedaref was fruitless, and even worse, led to new files being opened against us by the local police.

One evening we were stopped by a police patrol. The policemen pointedly demanded to know what the hell our business was in the area. Our cover story — searching for diving sites for hordes of tourists who were headed to the village — appeared to be satisfactory to them, but as they checked our papers and the box on the pickup truck, they surprised us by pulling out a Polaroid camera and taking pictures of our unshaven faces for the police archives.

Following the unsuccessful tour of Gedaref, it was decided to check the situation along the Sinkat-Erkowit axis about four hundred kilometers (250 miles) northeast of Gedaref. The road was narrow, poorly maintained and in fact led nowhere, unless you count the Erkowit recreation camp as "somewhere."

After driving just a few kilometers along this road, Danny and I finally found what we were looking for, a real godsend, or more precisely a British inheritance gift: an abandoned airfield.

No espionage agent skills were needed to identify the place as an airfield. Air force intelligence experts pointed us toward the site, having located an abandoned landing strip called Carthage on Sudanese maps. Several hundred meters to the right of the road a packed dirt runway could be seen, and on both sides, at regular intervals, we could easily spot the remains of concrete walls used as aircraft shelters. The runway, about a thousand meters long, was in prime condition, packed tight, with no potholes or trenches. The few torrential rains that had fallen in the area during the previous four decades since the first steamroller pressed it down had hardly left their mark. In short, super and meticulous work by the RAF. They may have called on the assistance of contracting firms from Palestine, such as the Jewish building company Solel Boneh.

This small airfield on the road to Erkowit was witness to fighting that raged here on one of the remotest battlefronts of World War II.

The story goes back to June 10, 1940. After the Nazi military machine succeeded in breaching the French lines and was already on its way to Paris, Benito Mussolini, Italy's fascist dictator, made the mistake of his life. Concerned he would lose out on the "fruits of victory," he abandoned his neutral stance, joined his spiritual disciple Adolf Hitler and declared war on France and Britain.

France capitulated to the Nazis. Stalin's Soviet Union was a Hitler ally, and French Communists were ordered by Moscow to be cordial to Wehrmacht soldiers who sat in the cafés of Paris. The United States stuck by neutrality, and the British, left alone in the battlefield, heard from their leader Winston Churchill that he couldn't promise them anything but "blood, sweat and tears."

Mussolini's declaration of war turned East Africa into another arena and caught the British in the continent off guard, to put it mildly. The Italian expeditionary force in Libya and other territories under Italian control placed Egypt and the Suez Canal, which was the British Empire's main traffic artery, at risk. The Italian garrisons in Ethiopia, Eritrea and Somalia dominated the naval access routes to the Red Sea, also threatening Sudan and other British colonies in East Africa. By August 1940, the Italians had taken British Somalia and started massing troops along the Ethiopia-Sudan border. This border ran a few dozen kilometers south of Erkowit and there the British hastily built a small airfield.

The East African front was rather a secondary one for the British general staff. But the British were in fear of protracted battles, perhaps due to the bitter experience they had on this front with the Germans during World War I. Then, a small German expeditionary force, less than a thousand strong, under General Paul von Lettow-Vorbeck, ran rampant between the years 1914–18 across all of East Africa, pinning down an army of hundreds of thousands of British, Indian, South African, Italian and Portuguese troops. Von Lettow-Vorbeck signed an armistice in November 1918, only after receiving confirmation that the battles in Europe were indeed over.

But the Italian army the British had to contend with after

Mussolini's declaration of war was made of a different stuff than the von Lettow-Vorbeck men. In January 1941, the British launched an all-out offensive on Italian East Africa, and within a few months liberated Ethiopia, Eritrea and Somalia.

The deserted airfield in Erkowit was a legacy of that forgotten war, the results of which included the return of Emperor Haile Selassie to his palace in Addis Ababa. The Ethiopian ruler, who carried the title "Lion of Judah" and at the time turned down an Israeli government request to let his Jews go to Israel, would help them now, albeit indirectly, to realize their dream of return to Zion on eagles' wings.

Chapter 33

Danny and I ran across the vestiges of this forgotten war later on as we toured the southern section of the Sudanese shoreline.

The air force requested that we check out a report that a battery of surface-to-air SAM2 missiles had been deployed in Tokar, not far from the border with Eritrea.

Compared to the pleasant weather atop the Erkowit range, the renewed encounter with the unbearable humidity of the coastal plain was a form of Chinese torture. I will never forget the trip to Tokar. Those living in the air-conditioning era will find it hard to imagine a ride of several hours in a red-hot jeep, with the windows wide open to catch a breath of moist air, all the while filling up with dust, because the road marked in red on the map was hardly a dirt track.

The coastal road terminates a few kilometers beyond Suakin, an old port city, south of Port Sudan. It was abandoned at the turn of the century for two reasons: the accelerated growth of Port Sudan itself and the blocking of the Suakin port because of overgrowth of corals. "Sleeping beauty" is the appropriate name for the town, whose hundreds of old but abandoned structures are made of coral stone. This is the reason that the town was recently added to UNESCO's World Heritage List.

The coastal road was constructed by the British, of course, as part of their preparation for attacks against Ethiopia and Eritrea. The road is very narrow, made up of concrete plates laid down on the sand. (In Palestine the British built similar roads, such as the concrete road that went to the ocean through the industrial zone of Herzliya, long before the entire area was covered with hi-tech plants and sumptuous villas.)

The original concrete plates laid by British army engineers some forty years ago between Suakin and Tokar did not hold up to the typical Sudanese neglect. From time to time the Toyota tires hit their remains. Most of the time, however, they just plowed through sand.

Our traveling speed did not exceed twenty kilometers (about twelve miles) an hour at best. In fact the road was nothing but two deep channels cut in the sand by the wheels of local Bedford trucks, with sand mounds in the middle.

The Bedfords had a high and wide clearance that enabled them to safely negotiate the middle mound. Our Toyota, however, laden with fuel and water as well as diving gear — to back our cover story — brushed nonstop against the ground.

We didn't give in, though, and after a long and grueling drive, despite the heat and difficulties, we reached our destination: Tokar. At the entrance to the town one couldn't but notice the missile battery. Vultures nested on the large radar dish. Two rusty missiles, still on their launchers, served as an improvised playground for the local children. The anti-aircraft position in Tokar, we told headquarters, need not bother the planners of the aerial rescue operation.

The town was a heap of hovels and several stone structures. The largest structure was of course police headquarters, whose main mission was to control the brisk smuggler traffic in the area. The main source of income for the local inhabitants was lively, though illicit, trade in alcoholic beverages made in Eritrea. The previous Italian rulers taught the locals the art of distilling brandy, other spirits and winemaking. The fact that grape vines are extremely rare in Eritrea didn't stop the production lines from grinding on for one moment. They apparently depended on commercial alcohol imported from other places.

I was reminded of a joke told about a winery that operated in the heart of Jerusalem's ultra-religious Mea Shearim community and produced a fine array of wines. On his deathbed, surrounded by his children, the proprietor told them: "My dear children. Come

closer, I want to let you in on a big secret." The grief-stricken prospective inheritors pricked their ears. "I would like you to know
that wine can also be made from grapes," he whispered to them,
and shut his eyes forever.

The spirits made in Eritrea were marketed in bottles adorned
with star-studded labels, as if they won every international competition. In any law-abiding country, they would be labeled "dangerous poison" along with a warning that sale was restricted only to
pharmacists and by medical prescription at that. They excelled in
particularly high alcohol content and led to instant intoxication,
horrible headaches and also to liver damage. To anyone used to
imbibing delicate wines with aristocratic labels such as Chateau
Lafitte, those spirits were a horror. Eritrean brandy was also known
as "Chateau Migraine" for the horrible headache — like a hammer
pounding on the temples — that was an inseparable part of the
drinking experience.

The heavy midday heat in Tokar chased even the toughest of
denizens to the few shaded spots in town. From there, they looked
with amazement at the two smiling white men who came to that
backwater of their own free will.

Chapter 34

The old Bedouin who sat on a small knoll not far from the deserted airfield on that hot night in May 1982 was sure he was dreaming. At the foot of the hill ran a cul-de-sac pointing in the direction of Erkowit. In the past, the number of cars traveling on that road could be counted on the fingers of one hand. That night, however, the area was teeming with activity the likes of which had not been seen since the distant days of World War II.

Truth is, I don't really know who was sitting on that hill, a Bedouin or a smuggler, old or young, but in retrospect we do know that someone was watching our activity at the Erkowit airfield, and also reported it to the police, albeit after we were done and had left the area.

Excitement overcame us ahead of the first aerial operation. We felt we were taking part in a historical event, a 1980s version of "On Eagles' Wings," the airlift of Yemeni Jewry to Israel in the 1950s. Even though we had all experienced adventures of various kinds in our lives, landing a heavy transport aircraft in the heart of a hostile country had not yet been featured on our resumes.

Collecting the "brothers" from the meeting place in the wadi went swiftly and efficiently. There were no special problems at police checkpoints, and the decision to switch to an aerial rescue spared us the need to reach the beach and crawl along dirt and mud trails on the way to some forgotten inlet.

The rusk and cigarettes method worked like a charm. The vehicles stood up to the task. The term "flat tire" did not appear in the logbook. Promptly after our arrival at the landing site, we started getting organized. The "brothers" were massed close to one of the concrete structures that once sheltered RAF Spitfire fighters from occasional strafing by their Italian adversaries. We checked the runway twice to be certain there were no obstacles or unexpected craters. We set down lanterns with faint lights at fixed intervals to mark out the runway. The pilots and navigators, equipped with night-vision goggles, detected the runway from a great distance, and the faint light from our lanterns also illuminated it well.

To make sure that we were alone in the area, two vehicles were dispatched to the road, north and south, to a distance of five kilometers (three miles) from the makeshift airfield. The single person in each vehicle was equipped with a two-way radio and plenty of patience.

We functioned like a well-oiled machine — quietly, efficiently and quickly.

The sky was clear. From time to time we could spot the faint flickering lights of an aircraft flying at high altitude, apparently on routine flights from Cairo to Nairobi or another destination. The passengers on that aircraft, cruising overhead at an altitude of thirty thousand feet, may have been sleeping in their narrow seats, absorbed in their immediate surroundings. The captain may have spotted an unidentified object on his radar flying at low altitude over the Red Sea, approaching the Sudanese coastline, but he probably didn't give it any undue attention.

Suddenly the radio came to life. Loud and clear a voice came over with a distinct Pinglish accent. The Hercules had crossed the coastline at low altitude and was approaching us. A deep sense of excitement gripped us. They would be here in a few moments. I lit another cigarette with shaking hands.

The scouts reported that the road was entirely deserted. No vehicle was moving at that late-night hour. Danny switched on the pickup truck headlights to signal the landing direction for the pilot.

"Identification good, I see you clearly, I'm descending," the pilot's voice was coming in clearly. We still couldn't see the aircraft, its lights switched off, and could barely hear its engines. But suddenly, a giant dark shadow appeared from the direction of the dark mountain range opposite us. It flew several meters above us, making us duck our heads instinctively like helicopter passengers fearing being hit by the rotor.

The aircraft touched down and was swallowed in the darkness. Then two things occurred simultaneously. A huge cloud of dust arose from the ground, and the deafening noise of four engines whose blade pitches were reversed in order to halt the huge metallic body tore through the silence. No one was able to hear our "Yahooooo" Indian-like battle cry, not even the anonymous onlooker monitoring the activity from his hideout. He probably thought that he was hallucinating or suffering the effects of multi-starred Eritrean brandy.

We drove onto the runway and raced toward the Hercules, which by now had reached the loading zone after a slow taxi.

The "brothers," massed behind a concrete structure, were scared to death, though you didn't need to be a Jewish farmer from a small Ethiopian village who had never seen an airplane before to have been awed by that Erkowit-style encounter in May 1982.

The C-130 engines were still working and the huge propellers kicked up tons of thin, annoying dust.

The loading bay in the Hercules rear section opened slowly. A small group of soldiers weighted down with two-way radios, assault rifles and even rocket launchers came running down the ramp. Danny started coordinating the boarding with the commander of the force and the captain of the Hercules transport.

Two soldiers and I, who had already worked as a team during training back home, ran toward a sand hill picked for observation and securing. While running, one of them handed me an Israeli-made Galil assault rifle. "What has this got to do with me?" I quipped. "I had my basic training in 1968. I can undo the gas plug on a Belgian-made FN rifle with my eyes blindfolded."

"Gee, you're old," the young man from the crack army unit responded promptly as he lay on a small sand hill in the heart of a vast desert. "Where are we, anyway?" he asked with excitement in his voice. He said that the only thing they were told during the briefing was that they were going to secure a covert immigration operation.

"Welcome to Sudan," I told the two. "If you walk for a few hours in that direction [I was pointing south] you'll reach Ethiopia."

I carefully surveyed the area. Nothing was moving, except for the white, bright cloud of dust that kept expanding by the minute. It could be spotted from a few kilometers away even without binoculars.

While the pair of soldiers kept their gaze in the direction of Ethiopia, lest we be surprised from there, I focused my binoculars in the direction of the aircraft.

Large crates were being removed from the aircraft and piled at its side. The unloading over, the "brothers" began boarding in small groups.

Observing them from afar, I wasn't aware of any difficulties. But later it transpired that they were terrified, and weren't happy at all, to put it mildly, to enter the huge metal body that descended on them from the skies with a horrifying noise, accompanied by clouds of thin dust that got in their eyes. Some tried to run away and got lost in the darkness. In the midst of the noise and dust it was also difficult to run a head count and make sure that no one was left behind.

Holding each other by the hand they walked up the loading ramp and were swallowed inside the belly of the large transport aircraft, illuminated with pale red light. "I felt like the prophet Jonah who was swallowed by a whale," recounted one of the "brothers" later, recapturing the moment he entered the aircraft.

On orders of the soldiers, including former Ethiopian immigrants who spoke Amharic, the "brothers" sat on the floor, crowded in between the piles of equipment. The medical staff, beefed up following the lessons of the recent naval evacuation, immediately began to check the passengers. There were young mothers with young babies tied to their backs wrapped in large pieces of cloth. These human bundles carried by their mothers always posed severe counting problems for us, because they did not appear different from bundles of clothes.

The older children and the young boys adjusted within seconds to the switch from the stone and donkey era to the aviation age. With wide-open curious eyes, they absorbed the goings-on, as did the men and several older dignitaries. One of them held a holy book that he had carried throughout the tortuous trek from a small village in the Gondar area. The "brothers" believed deeply that they were headed to Jerusalem, a city made entirely of gold. In the moments preceding takeoff, they weren't aware of the disappointments awaiting them in the Holy Land and what a gamut of humiliation, mostly at the hands of the orthodox establishment, they would have to endure before feeling like fully equal citizens of the State of Israel.

The loading took a long time. The Hercules engines were still running, and the huge propellers ground the dust-filled air. A faint red light broke from the cockpit. Through my binoculars I could see the crew sitting attentively, following the message traffic and checking the instruments to make sure that all systems were functioning well. Some of them wore night-vision goggles. I noticed that one of the pilots was looking in our direction, at the observation post the two soldiers and I occupied. I didn't believe that he could see us, but like a little boy, I raised my hand to wave at him. To my surprise, he waved too. To this day I wonder whether he responded to my gesture or reacted to something spoken in the cockpit.

At our securing point, the roar of the Hercules engines was very loud.

"How is it that no one hears the noise?" asked one of the soldiers as he was carefully scanning the darkened plain in front of us.

"My young man, we're in Africa, not in the Negev. This country is bigger than Germany, Britain and France put together. The nearest village lies tens of kilometers away, and they have neither electricity nor phones."

After a short while, which seemed like eternity, the codeword for breaking up the security detail came over the radio.

"That's it, we're going home. Look after yourselves," said one of the amiable soldiers. "And prior to the next time, do try to take apart and assemble a Galil rifle," he said as he took the gun away from me. "I personally signed for it," he added almost apologetically.

I was happy to ditch the rifle. I prefer taking part in operations that don't require the use of firearms.

The security team that had held the position on the other side of the runway arrived as well. The soldiers hastened to get on the loading ramp, which was still lowered. We surveyed the area for the last time to make sure that no "brothers" or soldiers were left behind.

Despite the dust-induced haze I managed to see the stunned faces of the hundreds of "brothers" crowded on the cabin floor. The loadmaster, who was responsible for loading, stood on the loading ramp and had time to bid us one last farewell before the door closed.

"Godspeed," Danny radioed the captain. The roar of the engines intensified. The cloud of dust became bigger, swelling to the size of an atomic mushroom.

The aircraft started racing down the runway, and then took off and disappeared into the darkened skies.

The roar of the engines remained audible for a little while longer, but soon the skies over Erkowit became silent again.

Chapter 35

The congratulatory cable we received from headquarters a few hours later was packed with kudos for our professionalism. "You made history," they wrote. "You brought 130 Jews to the country in an extraordinary way. Hats off, and success in the future."

We were delighted with the kudos, but what really warmed our hearts were the crates of equipment taken off the Hercules before the "brothers" got on board. There were dozens of brand-new air conditioners in original packing, and within a short period of time Gil, the technician with the golden hands, installed them in the bungalows at the village. They made the summer in the tropical hothouse that was Arous bearable.

The air conditioners were Israeli made, but bore no evidence as to their "kosher" origin. I don't know what pretext the Mossad buyers used when they asked for the manufacturer's labels to be switched when they ordered the machines. Israeli exporters have found varied ways to export their wares to Arab and Persian Gulf nations, but doubtlessly there exists no official document listing the export of several dozen air conditioners to Sudan. Today, I can divulge to the proprietor of the plant that supplied a bunch of air conditioners under the "Luxair" brand name (a Mossad invention) in 1982 that his products worked well in the harsh conditions of Arous, and that they may still be stuck to this day in the outer walls of the holiday village structures, serving as nesting places for ospreys or other birds.

Our local workers, who had learned not to ask unnecessary questions, treated with natural equanimity the fact that their crazy employers returned from Khartoum in a truck laden with shiny new air conditioners. We were not concerned that any official Sudanese body would try to investigate the legality of the imports, since such investigations were nonexistent in the Sudanese realm.

Another crate lowered off the transport contained an elongated body with a mast and fin: a windsurfing board purchased from Zvika, "King of Surfboards," in the old Tel Aviv harbor.

No doubt this was the first windsurfer ever seen in this part of the Red Sea. At its launch, all our employees gathered along the waterfront to follow the new Western invention with curiosity and amazement.

It's doubtful that even today they understand what message this contraption had for human development and seamanship. They are still wondering why someone needs to stand on a sailboat, why no panels are added to the hull, why the mast cannot be fixed as it should be and why there is no bench to make it easier on the sailor. Abu Medina, the veteran seaman, examined the new craft up close and it didn't appear likely that he was enthused by what he saw.

But this board, part of the first generation of windsurfer with a large fin in the middle and a triangular sail, gave the surfing enthusiasts in the group, myself included, hours upon hours of heavenly maritime pleasure.

In the morning hours there was constant wind in Arous which made going into and out of our lagoon a real child's play. To this day I cherish the memory of countless hours of fast surfing over a surface of water so clear and transparent that it was as though we were gliding in the air over a huge aquarium.

In the early 1980s, windsurfing was in its infancy. It was straight surfing without too many accessories, jumps, being harnessed to a trapeze and all those intricate tricks that characterize the sport nowadays. Anyone who knew how to sail was considered a surfer. The cynics among us quipped that anyone who could keep his balance and not fall into the water could be declared a winner. There is no need for anything except a floating body with a fin in the middle, a simple sail and a boom, the bar you use to control the sail, and that's that.

One day I had an exceptional experience, of the kind that

remains with you all your life. I went out on a morning surf in a light wind. I sailed along the coral reefs, following an osprey trying to descend on his breakfast. After getting far from the village, I was persuaded by the pleasant rays of the sun to switch to "total" sunbathing. I took my swimsuit off and hung it on the sail.

The soft rush of the bow of the windsurfer slicing through the water was more pleasant than ever before. The wind was blowing as if by special order with the ideal force and direction parameters.

But soon enough the idyll was shattered all in an instant. From the corner of my eye I spotted a huge shadow following the surfboard, not that of somebody standing between the sun and me, but an independent shadow that was moving stealthily beneath me. It had two large fins resembling giant wings, a very wide mouth bordered by two long lips, a black back, white stomach, and a long, sharp tail that moved slowly in the water. It was the shadow of a giant Manta ray, which is common in that part of the Red Sea.

I don't know how other fish and sea creatures relate to a windsurfer, but this Manta ray was particularly curious and attempted to check out the elongated, white object that sliced speedily through the water. With several powerful fin strokes, it overtook the windsurfer and started swimming alongside me.

The giant Manta ray is a harmless variety, feeding off plankton, tiny organisms that live in the water. But this piece of data left my mind the moment this specific specimen went into formation with the windsurfer I was standing on. My knees quaked at the sight of the Manta ray's gigantic fins, some two meters wide, moving slowly tens of centimeters below the windsurfer. A single strike from such a fin would send me flailing into the water, stark naked. Even if I screamed at Maria Callas's decibel level, there was no chance anyone could hear me along this isolated beach.

During those long moments of being accompanied by a Manta ray I vowed never to go out to sea without a small life jacket.

After a few minutes of close sailing, the Manta ray appeared to have lost interest in the long white object. It may have gathered that whoever I was, I had no interest in closer contact, and it disappeared the way it came — with several elegant strokes of the long fins, to be swallowed by the clear blue water.

It seems that this Manta ray spread the word among its friends that it was no use to court a surfboard, since despite the long hours of surfing I chalked up afterward, a small life jacket hanging from the sail for added safety, I never again had the experience of sailing in formation with a Manta ray.

Chapter 36

In retrospect, it seems to me that encounters of the Manta ray kind provide a partial explanation of the magic that Sudan operations held for us. There was an almost unbelievable combination of once-in-a-lifetime experiences — some deeply moving, like the image of little children playing in the wadi while waiting for darkness to fall and the operation to proceed, some entertaining like the Manta ray cruising majestically beneath the surfboard, and some dangerous, like the "Fridge Bay" incident — a blend of experiences that gave the sojourn in Sudan its unique, never-to-be-repeated flavor.

Stories were whispered in Mossad headquarters about the "sweet life" of the Sudan team. To be honest, I must admit that some of our experiences during these operations were certainly enviable. Indeed we were engaged in risky covert activity that included being shot at, being arrested and hunted, as well as exposure to exotic and potentially lethal diseases. But in between, we lived it up in one of the world's most beautiful spots. Ordinary people paid thousands of dollars to enjoy similar experiences, while not only did we not pay, but we were generously remunerated, in American dollars, a heartwarming arrangement compared with the problems of an average Israeli salaried worker in the early 1980s trying to cope with the effects of runaway inflation rates.

In addition to a basic salary deposited regularly in our bank accounts we also received a substantial per diem, personal risk bonus and various other payments hatched in the creative minds of savvy bookkeepers in the air-conditioned Tel Aviv office. We were even credited with an increment for drinks in an arid zone, even though all we had to do to quench our thirst was to mosey over to the refrigerator in the dining hall and pull out a can of coke, beer or cold tea.

So, it was a small wonder that the host of frustrated clerks at Mossad headquarters were jealous. They, whose last adventure was being stranded in an elevator due to a power failure, sat in their tiny rooms, reading thrilling reports that could have been taken from a Hollywood spy film. Additionally, the Mossad was then governed by a spartan code of conduct, a relic of the founders' era. Under this code it was permissible to spend huge amounts of money on operational needs, particularly an operation to save Jews. But whoever heard of purchasing a speedboat or a windsurfer at the expense of the Mossad, not to mention water skis, top-of-the-line diving suits and other gear? Month in, month out reams of invoices for purchases landed in Accounts and caused those in charge of disbursement to raise more than one eyebrow, fanning even higher the flame of rumors about "Operation Fun" in Sudan and the high-living atmosphere in the Arous Holiday Village.

This didn't bother us in the least. We continued to have a whale of a time as if on a vacation taken straight out of the pages of a fancy chromo catalogue of an elite travel agency.

At least twice a week we went on diving safaris to sites whose mere mention would induce phenomena akin to diver's vertigo among lovers of the deep. One site was the watery grave of the *Umbria*, a large Italian cargo ship that entered Port Sudan in the summer of 1940. On June 10, minutes before the captain gave the order to set sail for the next destination, Eritrea, British soldiers boarded the vessel.

"We are sorry to inform you," they told him, "that your government declared war on Britain and France a few minutes ago. You are under arrest as of now."

The Italian captain and his crew were of the patriotic variety and truly believed the fascist teachings of Benito Mussolini and the propaganda put forward by his regime about the Italians being the best of the world's warriors, and certainly the bravest of them all. This can be the only explanation as to why they decided to emulate the biblical Samson, who pulled the Philistine temple in Gaza down on himself. While the captain riveted the attention of the British officer with a series of vocal protests, his sailors opened the floodgates under the water line. The ship began taking water within minutes.

The British were furious. They tried to block the openings and save the *Umbria*, but then the Italian captain switched from shouting to explaining calmly: "My dear officers," he said, "the *Umbria* cargo includes seven thousand tons of landmines, artillery shells and ammunition for the Italian expeditionary army in Ethiopia. Besides flooding the boat, we also planted time bombs in the hold." Looking at his watch, he continued: "We have less than an hour left before detonation. You can imagine that when seven thousand tons of explosives go off, you will be able to strike the name Port Sudan off the map. We are patriots, but not suicidal. Believe me, the charges can be neutralized by seawater. And so, if you let us sink the boat, I promise there will be no explosion, and in return we shall not resist being taken prisoner."

The British couldn't decide whether to believe the insolent captain, but a quick check of the holds bore him out as far as the lethal cargo went. Fearing that the explosion and sinking of the ship in the center of the harbor would cripple any maritime activity, they decided to accept the Italian officer's version of the sixty-minute grace, move the *Umbria* out of the port and let it sink to its final rest in deep water. Its hold quickly filling up with Red Sea water, the *Umbria* thus set sail on its last voyage, which was very short and ended not far from the port, about forty meters below sea level.

Hans Haas, the well-known Austrian oceanographer and a father of underwater photography, visited Port Sudan in 1947, and spread the story of the *Umbria* throughout the diving community. He heard the story from Bill Clark, the British high commissioner, with whom he stayed. The governor told him that soon after the war, one Italian company sought his permission to send divers down to the wreck in order to extricate from it a treasure of half a million silver coins bearing the image of the Austrian empress

Maria Theresa, mother of Marie Antoinette, which had been des-
tined to pay the salaries of Ethiopians employed by the Italian
conquerors. The old Austrian thaler (the source of the word *dollar*,
incidentally) was for hundreds of years legal tender in Ethiopia.

British experts however ruled that the explosives on board the
Umbria were still active, and therefore the entire area around the
ship was cordoned off. Haas, who was quite naughty, ignored the
edict, dived in the forbidden site with his primitive camera and
returned with gorgeous photos that have since made the *Umbria* a
must for any self-respecting wreck diver.

In his book, *Under the Red Sea*, Haas describes his ground-
breaking dive into the wreckage, and how he succeeded in wrig-
gling through a door that already sported a colony of oysters and
corals, into one of the cabins of the sunken ship. "I saw on the
ceiling a beautiful lamp and I coveted it for a souvenir. I tried to
pry it loose, but failed," he wrote.

I don't know if Hans Haas is still alive, but one thing I am certain of: for years that lamp has been gracing the top of a chest of
drawers in the home of an Israeli citizen. The same fate is shared
by the beautiful copper bridge bell, a copper plaque inscribed with
the name *Umbria*, beautiful copper portholes and a plethora of
other items, all ending up during the 1980s in the homes of several
Israelis, veterans of the Sudan operation.

Nearly all those who took part in the operations were avid
divers, many of them former Navy SEALs, whom we nicknamed
SMBD's (acronym for Slow-witted Mine-Bearing Diver). Having
loads of free time, and access to the most sophisticated diving gear
between Eilat and the French navy base in Djibouti, "blue and
white" Israeli divers were often seen moving with steady flipper
action between the rusty, coral-encrusted corridors and store-
rooms of the *Umbria*. Sadly, we found no thalers, at least none
that I know of. Nor do I know of any Sudan operation veteran who
has significantly improved his lifestyle as a result of his sojourn in
that country.

Besides the *Umbria*, the Sudanese coastline is studded with

numerous magnificent diving sites. Abu Medina, the elderly fisherman who knew every reef along the coast, revealed another stunningly beautiful site to us. "We're going there," he said one day
pointing north with his hand. "A long, but most rewarding ride,"
he added.

Two Zodiacs were piled up with diving gear, extra fuel tanks,
water and some food. Abu Medina sat on the bow of the lead
Zodiac, and navigated between the reefs of the Sudanese coastline
like a Tel Aviv taxi driver in the morning rush. After two hours of
sailing, when we reached a reef that looked exactly like thousands
of others, he announced firmly that this was the place.

At a depth of several dozen meters we saw the elongated body
of a huge cargo ship. The winches were folded as though struck by a
powerful hand. On the white sand around the hull lay hundreds of
colorful boxes, or at least this is how they looked from the surface.
A closer look revealed that they were cars of every make and size.

The guys who dived to the site quickly established that the cars,
trucks, buses and other vehicles were vintage 1978 Toyotas. For
unclear reasons the ship, named the *Bluebell*, strayed dozens of
kilometers west of the international shipping lane and ran aground
on the largest coral reef located within sight of the Sudanese coast.
Its bow sliced the wall of the reef, stranded at the depth of some
twenty meters below water level. The stern rested on the bottom
of the sea, some eighty meters deep. The force of the impact sent
dozens of cars flying off the deck, smashing many others into piles
of twisted skeletons. Most of the vehicles, however, remained intact.
The ship itself suffered relatively minor damage. It lay upside down
in its entirety on the sea floor, to be enjoyed by the fish and other
dwellers of the deep. Barracudas chose to roam inside spacious
buses. Small sharks swam leisurely among the trucks and tractors,
and thousands of smaller fish, in all colors of the rainbow, moved
disinterestedly inside this immense artificial reef.

To my regret, for medical reasons mentioned previously, I was
forced to make do with observation from the surface with the aid
of a mask and snorkel. But even from this angle it was amazing

to see the guys diving onto the hull of this huge sunken ship, and into the dozens of cars scattered around it. Just like excited kids, they sat inside the cars, after making sure that no nervous moray eel was sleeping under the dashboard. Their feet, held inside large fins, did not exactly fit on the pedals, but this did not prevent them from playing at underwater driving, and the columns of air bubbles that emanated from the cars indicated that they were holding the wheel and producing driving noises.

Diving to the Toyota site was dangerous because of the difference of depth between the bow and the stern of the ship. While the bow had sunk to a reasonable level, diving to the stern or to the inverted bridge required meticulous planning of submerging and resurfacing in order to equalize pressures, preventing decompression damage and the phenomenon of divers' vertigo. But the Sudan team had an unusual concentration of top Israeli divers, from Navy SEAL veterans to civilian diving instructors who were active in the country at the time. Ruby, Shmulik, Ram Golombik, Louis, Gidi and the others knew full well that any diving accident in Sudan could be fatal because of the lack of proper medical care or equipment, such as a pressure chamber. Frolicking was certainly part of the spirit of the operation, but never during diving. As Ruby used to repeat time and again before going down, "Accidents don't just happen, they're caused."

There was also the beautiful reef around the Sanganeb lighthouse, as well as dozens of other diving sites that make the Eilat marine preserve at home look like a molehill at the base of Mount Everest. But despite all the fun there were downsides to living in Arous.

The heat during the day was unbearable. From time to time we were stuck with an emergency supply of water that sufficed just for drinking and cooking. Every minor health problem — see the case of my broken tooth — had ominous potential. Electrical power supply was as untrustworthy as Idi Amin's word. Entertainment, apart from sports or other self-initiated activities, boiled down to watching video films, subject to the availability of electricity.

You may recall that in the summer of 1982, the world soccer championship took place in Spain. To a bunch of young men stuck at the end of the world, this was a reason to celebrate. Sudanese television broadcasts from Khartoum could not be received at Arous. But Saudi Arabian television programs drifted easily over the Red Sea and found their way nicely onto our television screen. So we prepared ourselves for long nights of direct broadcasts from the green fields of faraway Spain.

Saudi Arabian television doesn't have to strain to win the title of the world's most boring station. The Saudi royal family, which became famous for the wild behavior of its sons at gambling and entertainment sites around the world, was overly concerned about the morals of its subjects. The programming included an overdose of historical serials about Mohammed and his successors, direct broadcasts of prayers in the Great Mosque in Mecca, animated children's films, nature films (as long as they didn't show copulating animals), and American serials which were brutally censored each time a bare-shouldered female peeked from the edge of the screen. Hugs and kisses, of course, were total taboo. But there were plenty of sports programs available.

We settled ourselves in for the first soccer game. And then, just before the start of the games, the screen went black. A junior prince had murdered King Faisal. "Forty days of mourning," said the caption on the screen, which gave way periodically to the face of a sad imam reading from the Koran. We vented our fury over the development by downing a number of beers and afterwards turned to finding a solution. Pulling together, we raised a tall iron mast atop which we attached an improvised antenna. We started zapping. Bingo: when the antenna pointed south the snowflakes disappeared. In their place appeared tiny images chasing a tiny ball. Additional fine tuning cleared up the picture.

I listened for a few moments and told my buddies that we were watching the North Yemen television station from Sanaa. Because of the distance the broadcasts were received in black and white, but we, alumni of the "color blotting" era of Israel television, accepted it with lenience. Even when the generator up and died again, we didn't throw our hands in the air. We recruited the small Honda mobile generator reserved for emergencies. And this was indeed an emergency.

Luckily for us, we were forced to watch only two or three Yemeni games. The Saudi leaders realized that persisting with the blackout policy would turn soccer lovers from friends to foes, and thus, inside less than a week the official mourning was reduced to a level that enabled direct broadcasts from Madrid, Valencia and Barcelona. In the meantime the Lebanon war broke out, which appeared decidedly bad on Saudi news shows. The fighting in Lebanon certainly had a direct impact on the IDF's and the Mossad's ability to allocate manpower and resources for the operation to rescue Ethiopian Jews. It temporarily went into deep freeze.

Our spare time was filled not only with diving, videos or soccer. From time to time we also took trips in the area. We had operational justification for these trips — checking out escape routes, all carried out with prior authorization from headquarters.

A nice touring destination was the old city of Suakin, located on a small island several kilometers south of Port Sudan. Suakin was known already in ancient times.

One legend has it that it was the meeting place of King Solomon and the Queen of Sheba. It is also mentioned in Roman era travelogues. An elderly merchant in Port Sudan told me yet another legend. He swore that it was the town's true story. "Thousands of years ago, when the monarchs of Egypt and Ethiopia were on good terms, the Ethiopian ruler dispatched a special gift to Pharaoh: seven beautiful virgins. The task of delivering them to Egypt was entrusted to the king's most loyal eunuch. During the trip northward, the eunuch wanted to make a stop at the island, which was totally deserted at the time. The denizens warned him not to come near the site, which was home to seven little devils. But the eunuch dismissed this as nonsense. When the contingent finally arrived in Egypt, Pharaoh was ecstatic, but soon his joy turned to anger when he discovered that someone had had his way with the virgins before him.

The eunuch swore up and down that no male had been spotted throughout the voyage, and that the only solution to the mystery was that the seven devils of Suakin Island had visited the virgins at night. The Egyptian ruler, in a spurt of generosity and forgiveness, released the eunuch and the virgins, but in order to confine the spread of rumors about the royal disgrace, forced them to live on the deserted island. And there, nine months later, the descendants of the virgins and the devils were born. "*Sawa jin* (the devils did that)," said the denizens, hence the name of the place: Suakin.

Until 1910 Suakin was the seat of the Egypto-British governor, but after the lagoon leading to the port became clogged and the Port Sudan port was expanded, all the residents left and it became a ghost town. Entry to the town was through a big white gate named after Lord Kitchener.

The buildings were built of white coral stone, replete with carvings and decorations. The most beautiful house had belonged to the family of the incumbent representative of the holiday village in Port Sudan, who had played host to Danny and myself in his home. All buildings in the town were destroyed or were on the verge of collapse, except for one which had served as an official guesthouse, and now sheltered the few policemen who were posted to the town to deter contractors from stealing the coral stones and smugglers from turning the small harbor into an operations center.

The ride to Suakin involved a "must" stop at the only café in Port Sudan, whose proprietor managed to produce small quantities of ice cream with a domestic ice-making machine. The ice cream itself was a disaster, but when one could only dream of Haagen-Dazs, frozen water with a dash of food coloring could easily be rated a delicacy.

I recall an agreeable trip to a small village, Mohammed Gol, which lies some one hundred kilometers (sixty miles) north of Arous. It was the place where Abu Medina's two wives lived, and was described by him as being particularly beautiful.

"We're going to your village," we told Abu Medina. "Do you want a lift?" He scrambled into the cabin even before we finished making the offer.

Traffic on the main north-south axis was incredibly sparse. The number of vehicles traversing this dirt track on any day could be counted on the fingers of one hand. But this didn't prevent the locals from parking themselves comfortably along the route, waiting to hitch a ride. They spent the long hours before the arrival of any truck dozing in makeshift booths to shelter themselves from the sun.

Several kilometers north of Arous, a tall man jumped out of such a booth and stood in the middle of the track believing that if there was room in the vehicle he could join the ride for a small fee. The local custom precluded leaving wayfarers by the roadside. About thirty years old, he didn't look like a local. He was surprised to see a bunch of Europeans in such a godforsaken place. "I'm a teacher by profession, Khartoum-born, and work at Mohammed Gol," he managed to tell us in broken English, gladly accepting our invitation to ride along.

I wanted to find out if he was happy to teach in such a remote place, or whether he had been sent here because he was the worst student in the teacher's college. I was also interested to hear what Sudanese children study in Mohammed Gol. But because of his poor English, the attempt to chat him up about the education methods in this part of the world failed.

The landscape along the way was stupefying. To the west there was a tall mountain range.

"Gold, much gold," the teacher explained, pointing at the mountains.

We, too, had heard about it from two geologists who came into the village one day saying they were working for a French company prospecting for gold in the mountains, based on the knowledge that primitive gold mines operated in this region in ancient Egyptian times.

Between the mountains and the ocean there was a desert plain, truncated here and there by isolated spots of green trees. To the east, the Red Sea shimmered.

We reached Mohammed Gol itself after several hours of rough travel that included swallowing a lot of dust.

The landscape was beautiful, but in contrast the village appeared pitiful: several wooden bungalows set around a not-too-large stone fortress resembling the observation posts set up by the Turks along the road from Jaffa to Jerusalem. (The remains of two of them can still be seen at the meteorological station junction outside Tel Aviv and at Shaar Hagai on the road to Jerusalem.) Around this fortress and between the shacks, the sand was littered with the remains of tens of thousands of large oyster shells, a testimonial to secret activity that went on here from 1905 to 1921, intended to establish a new and lucrative source of income for the British exchequer.

An eccentric British scientist, one Dr. Crossland, managed to persuade the British Home Office decision-makers that Mohammed Gol held the key to the production of cultured pearls. He claimed that in this very lagoon there were oysters that could be used for the controlled manufacture of cultured pearls, thereby seizing control of the growing market for fashionable pearl jewelry.

On orders from London, huge sums of money went into the project. The British navy took care of regular supplies of food and water, and an army of local fishermen brought Dr. Crossland the tens of thousands of oysters he claimed for his research. But the secret of raising cultured pearls was cracked by the Japanese, and Dr. Crossland had to abandon Mohammed Gol, as the Commonwealth office accountants engaged in financial juggling to bury the secret project's huge expenses in various other budget items.

The village was located at the edge of a beautiful lagoon, a group of rocks protruding from the water observable at its mouth. "*Umm girish* (mother of sharks)," Abu Medina cried out. "Sharks, a lot of sharks here."

This statement was borne out by a red-faced British man, about sixty years old, who came out of a large booth and was very happy to encounter European visitors. "I'm a fishing expert, here as a consultant to the Sudanese government," said the man, whose name I no longer remember. "Anyone hearing the name 'Red Sea' imagines water full of fish. But contrary to common wisdom, the Red Sea is not good for commercial fish harvesting. There are too many inedible kinds of fish, the contiguity of coral reefs doesn't allow net fishing, and the worst problem is the maintenance of cold storage depots for storing the catch. So what I'm left with is trying to improve the nutritional level of the people who live in the area."

On the beach sat a number of local fishing boats. Anchored in the water, however, was a European yacht, which appeared to be old and dilapidated. "This is where I live with my wife," the consultant said. The wife, about sixty too, noticed us from the deck. She went into a small boat and with quick oar strokes reached the shore. By her long black hair and features she appeared to be Asian.

"Real paradise, I'm not ready to return to rainy Britain," she said in a pleasant voice and with a smile, responding to a question whether she didn't miss civilization a bit. "Plenty of fish and lobsters, clean ocean, nice people," she said pointing at a windsurfer tied to the yacht. "I even have sport equipment, so what else do I need?" she said, breaking into hearty laughter that revealed white teeth.

Abu Medina, the elderly fisherman who had seduced us to travel to Mohammed Gol, alleging this was one of the most beautiful sites in Sudan, disappeared immediately into the bungalow of one of his wives. By the time our visit was over, including an idle chat and tea with the fishing consultant and his amiable wife, he also managed, despite his age, to visit his second wife as well as his offspring.

On the long way back to Arous, we reached the conclusion that the British fishing consultant at Mohammed Gol was certainly also a part-time spy, although we didn't manage to figure out what he was supposed to be reporting from Mohammed Gol and who really cared.

Another pretext for the spread of malicious rumors at headquarters about the wild living in the village was the arrival of the first tourists, real tourists! These were tourists of the kind that seek exceptional thrills in the classified ads of divers' magazines, in which we took care to publicize the reopening of the Arous Holiday Village.

The tourists, mostly Dutch and German, were very easy to accommodate. They came in small groups, up to six divers in one go, and paid a fortune to spend a week in one of the least traveled and least dived spots in the world. They had no high expectations. They knew that for the privilege of surfing over virgin reefs, one has to pay not only in money but also in nerves. Therefore they covered a tough trek starting with obtaining entry visas to Sudan. Flying there was also complicated.

To lower the cost of tour packages, our representatives reached a deal with an East European airline to bring the tourists to Khartoum for a not-too-large sum of money in cold capitalist cash. Arriving at the Sudanese capital was only one step on the road to happiness. The tourists also faced a domestic flight to Port Sudan on "Inshallah Airways" and a bone-racking trip in a Toyota along the dirt track leading to the village. Going back, they had to contend with the same track in the opposite direction. No wonder, therefore, that the tourists knew how to appreciate the service we offered them in the middle of nowhere on the Red Sea coast: three to four dives a day, professional divemasters, first-rate gear including tank refills, tasty fresh food, a bottle of cool beer on the open veranda at night, and even air conditioners that functioned for several hours every day.

The village's fame reached the foreign diplomats in Khartoum and some of them began coming to the village in a thin but steady trickle.

Since Sudan is an unconventional country, some of the visitors were not of the usual variety of holiday-village frequenters, such as British commando officers, for instance.

"One morning, when the village was empty of tourists, some mysterious images emerged from the desert," a village crew member recalled in later days. "They were dressed in a hodgepodge of local clothing and military uniforms, and carried huge rucksacks on their backs. The guests introduced themselves as 'British extreme tourists,' but it was immediately clear to us that they were professionals. Indeed it turned out later that they were members of the British SAS elite unit sent into the Sudanese desert on a survival exercise. They asked to be put up in one of the outer, abandoned structures. There they whiled away their time resting, joined us on diving and fishing trips and enjoyed every moment.

"Some time later, watching television documentaries about the arduous training of this unit, it became clear to me that they were fibbing big time. They were supposed to survive in the desert, catch lizards, look for water and open their emergency rations only as their last resort. They survived very well with us. It's a pity we couldn't monitor their fake radio communications briefing their commanders about their toils in the scorching Sudanese desert. It would have been interesting to find out if their commanders became wise to this, and whether they concluded the drill with flying colors. Go figure."

To ensure the well-being of our guests, we boosted the workforce crew with a number of Eritrean women, who were in charge of room service, including cleaning and laundry. Some of them provided sex services to the local employees. I hope I won't damage the polished image of Mossad employees by noting that at least one of its tenured officials occasionally abandoned his body to a "massage with sexual gratification," Eritrean-Sudanese style.

The diving and touring exploits were immortalized in photos. For appearances' sake, the flow of visitors to the village was increased by some senior Mossad officials who came over in the guise of visitors. On going home, they gleefully reported on the typical recreation and tourist routine at the village. In no time, photos of Sudan team members in perennial vacationer postures were passed from hand to hand in the hallways of the office in Tel Aviv. Rumors of sleaze and corruption were flying from one room to another and from one screen to another giving the Sudan operation a reputation for being an endless orgy.

Chapter 37

We never went back to the old British landing site at Erkowit for the simple reason that someone, perhaps that old Bedouin, or an anonymous goatherd, took the trouble of informing Sudanese authorities of the unusual activity that went on there on a summer night in 1982. Sudanese investigators who arrived in the area found a great deal of evidence of that activity, from the clear, crisscross tracks of vehicles to the near commercial quantities of empty cans of Lipton Ice Tea.

No doubt this was a major operational blooper. Because of the heat, we availed ourselves of cartons of the refreshing drink that happened to clutter the shelves in the Indian supply store in Port Sudan. These cans told Sudanese investigators that the unknowns who traipsed around the Erkowit dirt runway were foreigners. Local Sudanese don't drink cold tea, and certainly not from cans that sell at exorbitant prices by local standards. It was reasonable to assume that they were up against a bunch of sophisticated arms smugglers who delivered war materiel by air to the Eritrean and Tigrean underground movements. They may have even suspected us, but never called on us.

The Mossad found out about the investigations in Sudan regarding Erkowit, and promptly issued an order to make sure to comb the area well after the end of future operations, removing any scrap of evidence. Since Erkowit was now in the sights of the local security service, an alternate site had to be sought, closer to Gedaref.

For the air force, moving closer to Gedaref meant special preparations and a new ball game. Unlike the easy approach to the abandoned Erkowit landing site, which was close to the sea and involved a short and relatively safe section in Sudanese air space, a deep penetration into Gedaref included penetrating Sudanese air space from the north at low altitude, and over two hours of on-the-deck flying, including challenging dark night navigation problems, and all this in the pre-GPS era.

To the people on the ground, however, it meant a mini-revolution: a relatively short ride after collecting the "brothers," breaching one roadblock, maybe two, and completing the mission from pickup time to the dispatch of the "brothers" to Israel within one night.

Along with the operational decision to deepen the aerial activity inside Sudan, headquarters decided to refresh the command team to adjust to the new conditions.

Danny, the courageous field man whose resourcefulness gave birth to these operations, the unstoppable force who would persist until he moved the unmovable object, was no longer suited to be in charge of operations that had grown ever more complex. He was an improvisation and quick-fix master, but a disaster as far as planning was concerned.

In retrospect, it appears that it was a miracle that the first operations went off without tragic incidents. The time we were under his command could be summed up as the "without era." We set out without spare parts, without spare tires, without a backup plan for emergencies, where and how to get away. And this is only a partial list. We attributed the fact that these operations ended successfully, despite occasional incidents, to divine protection thanks to Danny's purple skullcap, which remained behind and didn't feel the rigors of the Sudanese sun. And now, in light of the new operational circumstances, there was a need to set up an extensive infrastructure to cope with the host of problems involved in such a complex operation.

One must remember that Danny had been involved in the Sudan affair since 1979. Even Superman would have shown signs of weariness after such a long period of action. Danny was therefore promoted to an operational job in Europe that also enabled him to spend more time with his family. After acrimonious and bitter wrangling at headquarters, a new commander was named: my friend and buddy Yariv.

Yariv was the chief instructor in the course I took in the fall-summer of 1974–75. We had kept in touch since. Yariv had an entirely different approach from Danny's. But he, too, was one of the very few who turned the Israeli Mossad (Institute) for Intelligence and Special Operations, as the Mossad is known officially, into an espionage agency that can do the impossible.

I remember one surrealistic evening in the garden of the home of a Sudanese cabinet minister in mid-1984. The minister felt his way in the dark to the edge of the lawn to locate the stash of whis-key bottles he had buried under the lawn. The ruler Jaafar Nimeiri's position was weakening. Seeking to placate the extreme Muslims, he decided to impose the Islamic religious Sharia laws across Sudan. In front of television cameras, a big steamroller crushed all the beer and whiskey supplies of the Khartoum Hilton into a pile of tin and glass.

All of a sudden, alcoholic beverages disappeared from the stores, and anyone seeking a drop of alcohol (the name originated from Arabic, incidentally) had to rely on contacts on the black market and mentally prepare for a huge financial expense. Thus we found ourselves savoring the forbidden drink, which the minister, despite his loyalty to Nimeiri, was forced to pull from its under-ground stash in the garden to serve three distinguished European guests.

The three — Mickey, Yariv and myself — were longtime bud-dies. Mickey, a brilliant doctor, a former platoon commander in the crack "Egoz" unit, and Yariv, had both married women from my old neighborhood. I knew Mickey from high school, and only a few days earlier the three of us had lounged on deckchairs in the community swimming pool, swapping stories. Now we were lounging at a different poolside, each with his own alias, choking on the warm whiskey of a Sudanese minister.

"What for life," Yariv sighed, mimicking the mock French

accent of Peter Sellers in the role of the helpless Inspector Clouseau in the Pink Panther films.

This definition was appropriate to Yariv's fascinating life story, which deserves some elaboration. His English-born mother came from one of the most respectable families in Manchester. Her brother achieved the prestigious title of Queen's Councillor, and was a member of the House of Lords, hence Yariv's "Lord Yariv" nickname. A few days after the end of World War II his mother met a young British army officer who was born in Tiberias and fell into Nazi captivity in Greece in 1941; at the end of the war he was sent back to England to recuperate. The two fell in love. Yariv was born in 1947.

A year later the Israeli War of Independence broke out, and his father, who was considered one of the brightest officers in the fledgling IDF, died in battle in the Galilee. The young widow went to England with her son for a few years, which explained Yariv's British accent. But in accordance with the father's will, which asked that his son be educated in Israel, they returned to Israel when Yariv began first grade. She moved to Haifa, remarried and had another son.

Yariv began his military service in a non-combat unit because he was an orphan of a serviceman and graduated an intelligence officer training course. On graduation day, he went south, and into the office of Amos Yarkoni, the legendary Bedouin commander of the "Shaked" desert reconnaissance unit, removed his officer's insignia and asked to join. "I want to serve under you as a rank and file soldier," he said, and was accepted. Weeks later, after proving his worth, he regained his officer's status.

After demobilization, Yariv was one of the first flying security men on El Al airliners, and in no time was recruited to the Mossad operational unit and was regarded as a rising star. A framed testimonial buried deep inside a drawer in his home proclaims him as one of the recipients of the "Israel Defense Award." His rise to the top was halted because of his signing off on the Letter of the

Ten and the ensuing petty mudslinging campaign by his rivals as though he had been brought up on petty smuggling charges.

A furious Yariv promptly left the Mossad and at age twenty-eight was accepted into an air force pilot training course, completed it successfully and was posted to a Skyhawk squadron. A mechanical fault in a Skyhawk jet fighter he was flying brought Yariv's aviation career to a sudden end. He was forced to bail out of his burning aircraft, flying at low altitude, and was seriously injured. He still suffers from neck and lower back problems. Despite his injuries, he was offered a post in the air force flying transport aircraft, but Yariv, who had always demanded the most of himself, quit his flying career and returned to civilian life.

He learned a new profession — computer programming — and tried to control his raging adventurous spirit. Then Mossad headquarters decided to replace Danny, who was leading the Sudanese operation, with someone with a proven operational record and broad aviation experience. Yariv was a natural choice. The moment he was approached, he said yes.

Yariv and Danny's overlap period went well. The two were well acquainted from Yariv's previous tour in the Mossad. Both were signatories to the famous letter, and occasionally participated in the same operations. But over the years a deep chasm of hate opened up between the two men.

Years after the operation of bringing the Ethiopian Jews to Israel was completed, both Danny and Yariv quit the Mossad, slamming doors behind them. It was pretty typical of the organization as it became increasingly institutionalized to lose many of its "crazy" workers and other "troublemakers," including some Hafisniks, in favor of straitlaced and docile clerks. Danny was lucky to retire at a relatively young age, mostly thanks to his glorious operational record, which balanced out bloopers he committed during his last years of service that could have cost him a dismissal with disgrace.

Chapter 38

Yariv's approach to the Sudanese operations was totally different from Danny's "no worries" stance. It was characterized by no-nonsense professionalism and thorough and meticulous planning.

Now, the Ethiopian Jews rescue operation assumed a welcome and well-planned routine. Were it not for the secret aspect, one might think that a travel office specializing in extreme tours was at work.

Despite Israel's continuing embroilment in the Lebanese quagmire, the landings of air force Hercules transports was stepped up. The air force transport squadrons welcomed these extraordinary operations that conferred on the pilots an aura of battle and whetted their appetite for adventure. They were hungry for more. In the years 1983 and 1984 there were nights when three Hercules transports landed in Sudan in succession, loaded up hundreds of Jewish refugees and flew them directly to Israel.

Yariv's era, however, was not totally trouble free. For instance, there was an elderly woman who ran into the desert, frightened by the roar of engines. She reached Israel only in the following operation a few months later. There was also a SAM2 missile fired from an active Sudanese army position at an air force Hercules that was heading toward us. We clearly saw the missile trail slicing the night's dark skies. The Sudanese fired it directly at the aircraft, as if it were a cannon shell. It stands to reason that trouble in the missile radar system was the cause of the firing. The Hercules pilot was not overly concerned and landed safely on the improvised landing strip. There were violent incidents as well: forcible breaching of police roadblocks because an officer insisted on looking through the contents of the trucks — a pretty frightening experience, despite our childish and unfathomable delight on seeing the barrier drums scatter in every direction, prompting the surprised policemen to take cover. And there was a more dangerous incident, where the policemen, against all odds, managed to collect themselves and started chasing the fleeing convoy. Lucky for the escapees, the policemen abandoned the chase after a few kilometers because of a mechanical failure.

There were endless technical problems, which under Danny could have stalled the operation. To wit, three flat tires in succession. This time, though, unlike the past, each vehicle was equipped with two spare tires and an appropriate tire-changing kit. So, except for a slight delay in the original schedule, no operational damage was incurred.

In another instance, although too many "brothers" reached the pickup point, it was decided to take them all aboard. In the end the side panel of one of the trucks came undone, and people fell out of the vehicle. Fortunately, the umbrella of miracles that shielded the operation under Danny had been handed over to us, at least partially, and no one was hurt.

The holiday village operation also became blissfully routine. Thanks to a massive input of funds from state coffers, the Mossad team managed to realize the dream of the Italian entrepreneurs who built it in the 1970s, and the Arous Holiday Village became Sudan's foremost recreation site.

For the smooth daily running of the village, women were recruited in Israel with an appropriate background and an ability to stick to a cover story. Until its closing down in the spring of 1985, it was run alternately and high-handedly by Ilana, Gila and Yola. Each had her own management style, but in all it was a success story that made it possible for the village to operate efficiently in every instance and provide the appropriate cover for the rescue operation. When crew members drove out to "bang Swedish nurses in Kassala" or "fetch new equipment from Khartoum," the women remained in the village with one or two other workers, thereby ensuring its smooth running.

The presence of Ilana, Gila and Yola breathed a fresh, cool wind into the Wild West atmosphere that characterized the place prior to their arrival. Yola even met her future husband during the operation.

The initiation problems at the village had completely disappeared. The drinking water problem was solved with the aid of an Israeli-made compact, sophisticated desalination system, flown in by a C-130 Hercules transport one night, that produced several hundred liters of high-quality drinking water a day. Simple improvisation provided hot running water for the showers — harnessing the scorching Sudanese sun to heat up water in a large metal container painted black.

After many hours of hard labor, Gil, the technician, overcame the generators' maintenance ills and restored them to their pristine state. Electricity supply was restricted to several hours a day: from noon time till evening, enough to keep the food refrigerators in the kitchen reasonably cold, the desalination and water pumps running and the air conditioners operating at the height of the scorching heat. The silencing of the air conditioners for the rest of the day won overwhelming support from the tourists and visitors, who soon learned to enjoy the sounds of silence typical of the area.

One of the tourists who came to the village was a Canadian, head of one of countless Western aid groups that worked at the time in Sudan. He would go on trips to the coral reefs, marvel at the sights, and ask questions continuously. One day he went to sea accompanied by Ram Golombik, the diving instructor. When their Zodiac was out of anyone else's hearing range, the Canadian turned to Ram and said, "I know you are Israelis." Ram nearly fell overboard with surprise, all the more so because the Canadian was speaking in fluent Hebrew.

It turned out that this Canadian was part of a private rescue operation on behalf of a North American Jewish aid outfit. Its activists had reached the conclusion that the Jewish people and the State of Israel weren't doing enough to rescue the Ethiopian Jews languishing in Sudanese refugee camps. One method they

adopted was smuggling Jews in small aircraft to neighboring
Kenya, an escape route which was discontinued after one of the
airplanes crashed and its passengers were detained for extended
interrogation. Overall, their actions in Sudan were amateurish, and
their presence, which caused Sudanese security services to increase
their vigilance, hurt our own rescue efforts.

How did the Canadian find out that the village operators were
Israelis? "For a long time I've suspected that this village serves as
an Israeli forward base. Final confirmation came when I watched
the crew prepare breakfast. Only Israelis cut their salad vegetables
so thin," he said.

To his credit, it must be said that he kept his findings to himself, and shortly after the plane crash and some conversations with
"appropriate elements," the heads of his group became convinced
that the best way for them to contribute to the well-being of the
Jews would be focusing on financial assistance, improving sanitary
conditions in the refugee camps and leaving the covert activity to
Mossad pros.

Business at the village was thriving. So were the earnings. "The
Mossad accountancy is built to handle losses," quipped one senior
official. "What would happen if we started making money? How
can we enter it in the books?"

Now the flow of money created management problems of a
different kind, including suspected withholding of funds and
mismanagement. There was one case of a large sum of money
"disappearing" which was investigated. But as far as I know, the
circumstances remained unclear even after the probe, and the
atmosphere in the office, particularly among some of the crew who
were allegedly involved, remained sour.

Groups of tourists from Europe were coming in a more or less
regular fashion. To members of the Khartoum diplomatic community, the village became a desirable spot for weekends or short
vacations, and prior booking was required on particularly packed
dates.

The communications problem with Khartoum was solved by a

modern radio network that linked the village to the company office in Khartoum. And so the administrators were able to properly run the purchase of food and prepare for the arrival of guests.

Officially, permits for radio network operations were required by the Sudanese Postal Authorities and the military. We got around the problem by installing an impressively large communication console in the suite of one of the most senior administration officials, and possibly by making a small contribution to the "orphans fund" he ran. During one of our routine visits to Khartoum, Gil the technician and I were sent to check out the console. While Gil rummaged through its intestines, I sat in the minister's chair, surveying the world from the point of view of a Sudanese general, a member of the ruling military junta, and I must confess I rather enjoyed it. Strangely enough, at the time I was already a *Maariv* staff member.

Chapter 39

In the fall of 1982 I left the Mossad for the third and nearly last time. My special contract ended. Because I drew much satisfaction from the work in Sudan, I sought to extend it and perhaps even rejoin the Mossad, but the idea fell through because of stiff opposition by the head of the Mossad manpower division, which didn't favor employing a worker who came and went too frequently.

I again signed various demobilization papers, handed back equipment, took my severance pay, took leave of my many friends and strode into civilian life. A good friend introduced me to Yisrael Peled, an energetic young man, a former IBM employee who was dreaming of setting up an empire of computer magazines. For several months I was privileged to serve as editor-in-chief of *Anashim Vemachshevim* (People and Computers) and *Machshev Ishi* (Personal Computer) magazines. At the same time I served as producer on the morning news show of Kol Israel radio in Tel Aviv. But the computer world was not my cup of tea, and therefore this chapter in my life ended. I took leave of Peled, who is today the proud proprietor of a mini empire of computer magazines.

Since throughout my life chance has taken me in interesting directions, I wasn't at all surprised that in early 1983, following a meeting with Tami Guy, an old friend, I ended up on the foreign news desk of *Maariv* newspaper, and have been there ever since. In the meantime I re-married, and shortly afterward found myself in Sudan again, this time as a "reservist." Like any average Israeli I was called up for the annual one-month service in the army. But in my case, somebody in the Mossad pulled some strings…

"Welcome back," I was greeted with a smile in my old Mossad unit.

"We knew you'd be back. Your goings away are always tempo-rary…" said the female clerks.

The truth is that there was something addictive in participating in the operations to rescue Ethiopian Jews. We were a bunch of twenty to thirty Israelis who worked on Sudanese soil in operations that took place between 1981 and 1985. Many of us have remained in touch, getting together once every few years in nostalgic, "those were the days" style.

So, I was up on things that had occurred in the intervening period from my resignation in the fall of 1982 until I returned to active service. Besides encounters with old buddies, I gleaned a lot of information from the "censor's tray" — the small tray to the right of the night editor, where I could find copies of news stories sent in the evening for approval by the military censor and their new, shorter versions published in the morning in the paper, dictated by those who were supposed to know what is good or bad for Israel's security.

In the early 1980s military censorship was much more powerful than today, and thus anyone seeking to get a full picture of what was really happening in Israel in those days of the Lebanon war could find it only in that small tray.

In principle, I'm no fan of censorship, except in very clear-cut cases concerning human lives, such as prior reports about IDF troop movements, or details about a covert operation carried out by the State of Israel in faraway Sudan, with the lives of Ethiopian Jews at stake.

In 1983, the Arab and international press started running first reports about the movement of Ethiopian Jews to Israel. Israel opted to totally ignore the reports, and rightly so.

At the same time, strict censorship was imposed on all Israeli media and Israeli-based foreign press corps concerning any report linked to the immigration of Ethiopian Jews. However, it must be noted that the number of those privy to the secret shot up expo-nentially with every immigrant who arrived here. Handling the immigrants were the big and cumbersome Jewish Agency network, the Ministry of Immigrant Absorption, the Ministry of the Interior, the Ministry of Health, local authorities, Wizo, Naamat women's organization and God knows who else. To the credit of the journalists, particularly the foreign correspondents, they kept silent despite the wealth of information that swelled their briefcases. They knew full well that prior publication could bring about the collapse of this humanitàrian rescue mission.

The media explosion was preceded by a long gestation period that ended because Jewish Agency heads had an urge to shoot their mouths off. The subject made headlines in January 1985, because of a Jewish settler magazine and a senior Jewish Agency official. More about this later.

All the reports about the Ethiopian immigration filed by *Maariv*'s industrious reporters, mainly from Ashkelon, Afula and Atlit, where the new arrivals were concentrated, were sent straight to the censor's tray. Foreign wire service reports concerning this immigration, originating in Sudan or other countries, also went through the tray.

It was thanks to this tray that I kept abreast of developments, and had learned from my Mossad buddies that the operation was continuing. Thus I found out that in the fall of 1982 and winter of 1983, more seaborne operations had taken place — in the familiar but not so desirable style of the "Fridge Bay" incident. The number of "brothers" brought over in these operations was small. Considering the high level of risk involved, it was decided to resume the aerial option. As chance would have it, the decision was made during the time I returned to service in Sudan.

In those days, the overzealous actions of some senior Mossad officials and their close ties to the leaders of the Lebanese Phalangist party caused Israel to become embroiled in the Lebanese quagmire. I was content with my good fortune that instead of serving as an intelligence officer in bleeding Lebanon and attempting to undo the tangle wrought by the "Phalangist lobby" in the Mossad, I dealt with the prettier aspect of the Mossad activities — saving the hungry and desperate Beta Yisrael refugees.

It seems to me that I was the first, and probably last, journalist who participated in a scheduled Mossad operational activity, and over a period of time. I imagine that one of the reasons I was recruited to serve in Sudan, despite my being an active journalist, was the fact that the commanders were convinced that I made a complete distinction between civilian activity and my own security role.

The operational team in Sudan didn't make much of my "journalistic" presence, since most of them were civilians who were drafted into action for set periods of time, and were not affected by the phobia plaguing some Mossad heads, who hasten to put their guard up as soon as they hear the words "journalist" and "press."

That tour of duty, which officially was in the framework of army reserve service, was certainly exceptional. A day after being recruited, I was already on my way to Sudan. Three days later, at the same time my colleagues in the *Maariv* newsroom were checking the incoming news wires (those were the last days before computers took over newspaper offices) for news coming from Africa about the harsh hunger prevailing there, I was driving a doorless "Sudanese" truck, breaching police roadblocks and loading Beta Yisrael immigrants onto air force transport aircraft in the middle of the desert.

Besides actively taking part in operations, I was called upon from time to time to accompany new recruits on their first mission to Khartoum. For instance, I had the pleasure of flying there with Mickey, my childhood friend. Mickey had many positive attributes, which prompted Yariv to name him his deputy. In his military career he was a platoon commander in the "Egoz" reconnaissance unit, more than once proving he could keep his cool in stressful situations. He had a tremendous sense of humor that came across even in French, a language he had mastered at a mother-tongue level during long years of study in Belgium.

He is also a fine doctor. Several minutes into our flight to Khartoum, Mickey listened attentively to a series of coughs produced by a Sudanese who sat in the row in front of us. "This week

I treated a tuberculosis patient, and my diagnosis is that this passenger too has TB," he whispered. "We had better get away from him to avoid the risk of contracting the disease. Let's move a couple of rows back."

This period was interspersed with amusing incidents. At the height of a landing drill for Hercules transports in the Negev, a film crew got off the aircraft headed by Menashe Raz, a TV producer. In retrospect, it emerged that the air force history division had decided to document the historic Sudan operation. It sent a crew with special night shooting equipment to film the pre-operational practice as well as the operation itself. The task was entrusted to Raz, who was a reservist with the Air Force Operations Department documenting unit.

I had met Menashe in my Jerusalem and Kol Israel days. But during that cold night in the Negev he looked at me several times as if trying to place me on his recollection map. On the other hand, I was honor bound to the Mossad security officer who made me swear by all that we held dear not to get near newsmen. That night I invested a goodly part of my energy not just in landing a heavy military transport, but also in dodging Menashe Raz and the infrared cameras of his film crew.

Besides my wife, the only person who knew what I was really up to was my boss in the newspaper, Ido Dissenchik, who later became the paper's editor-in-chief.

On the eve of my second "reserve duty" departure for Sudan, I sought a meeting with Ido. I decided on this move because of my familiarity with the Mossad management system. Despite the prevailing wisdom that they were guided only by the "good of the state and operational considerations," I knew that the senior Mossad officials were also driven by intrigues, power struggles and rear-end covering phenomena that dominated the organization.

Ido was a member of *Vaadat Orchim*, the Editors' Forum, which in the 1980s gave the chief editors of the Israeli media access to occasional secret briefings, "for their ears only," not for publication, so I knew he was not in the dark concerning events in the Sudan. "I know that you are up on everything concerning the immigration of Ethiopian Jews from Sudan," I told him. "I know the organization that is sending me there through and through, and only God knows what story they will release in case of a mishap or disaster. I want you to know the truth."

Ido's eyes widened in disbelief when I described to him where I was going to spend the next thirty days. He smiled from ear to ear. He seemed to like the almost surrealistic idea that a *Maariv* journalist was taking part in a covert Mossad operation. He promised to hold his tongue, and approved my leave, although the frequency with which I was summoned for operational duty wrecked the news desk's work schedule.

One day, as I was traipsing somewhere between Gedaref and Port Sudan, the phone rang in my home in Israel. The caller identified himself as a member of a jury panel that had decided to award me the first prize in a competition among computer journalists. Something had come out of the brief period of my dabbling in the computer world after all. The award came with a sizable monetary prize and the organizers expected that the recipient would collect it in person, acknowledge the award and possibly deliver a short speech.

"I'm terribly sorry," my wife said. "I'm sure Gadi will be happy to take part, but he is doing his reserve duty now and it's not at all certain he will be able to participate."

"What's the problem?" the caller responded. "Isn't he an officer? Let him arrange a few hours' furlough for himself, get in a jeep and come. For all I care, he can show up in uniform, as long as he makes it to Beit Sokolov at 11 am on Friday."

To my wife's credit, it must be said that she didn't lose her cool. "I'm still very, very sorry," she said. "Gadi is an intelligence officer and this reserve duty stint is different than usual. He went on a long voyage with the navy, and they are expected in Haifa only in ten days' time."

That Friday, my mother and wife went up to the podium at Beit

Sokolov in Tel Aviv and received the award on my behalf for the better glory of the cyberworld and its future impact on humanity. At that very moment I was struggling with Louis, Mickey, Dudu and Yariv to pull out a truck caught in deep mud on the edge of one of the remotest areas of one of the world's poorest countries.

Chapter 40

The living room of the Sudanese businessman was pleasantly shrouded in darkness. The air conditioner in the wall produced a monotonous humming noise. Both combined to plunge the room into blissful coolness, enough to disguise the 41-degree (about 106 Fahrenheit) weather outside.

Three European men were waiting for the host, who specialized in rental of fairly new vehicles, in pretty good condition and at exorbitant rates by European standards, but very reasonable by comparison with the levels of service and the car fleets of his competitors.

The lengthening wait offered a chance for the three Europeans, ensconced in a small room in this godforsaken place so far from home, to engage in small talk.

"What are you doing here in Khartoum, if I may ask?" inquired one of them, a tall, bespectacled man in his mid-forties, speaking English with a slight Canadian accent.

"Nothing out of the ordinary," responded the other man, several years younger than the inquirer, in British English, and with natural frankness. "I'm a spy," he continued.

"Interesting," said the Canadian. "And who do you work for?"

"For the Israelis. I am an Israeli spy," answered the younger man.

"I hope for your sake that this is not only a fascinating job but also a profitable one," continued the Canadian nonchalantly, and went back to the old newspaper he had been reading.

This polite conversation nearly caused the third man to have a heart attack. With each new word, he sank deeper into the padded floral armchair without uttering a sound, while his complexion became closer and closer to the whitewashed wall behind him.

"You're nuts, you're insane, totally off your rocker," he screamed at the "Israeli spy" in a shrill voice the minute they ended their meeting with the Sudanese businessman and drove away in their rented Toyota. His name was "H," a senior Israeli Air Force pilot, sent to Sudan with a veteran field person, to make sure that the new landing strip near Gedaref conformed to the requirements.

"I was told that you are brave and cool as a cucumber. But everything has a limit," he continued screaming at the "Israeli spy," who was none other than Yariv. "To blow your cover like that, even as a joke, in front of a stranger is not courage, it's suicide! Do you want to ruin the whole operation? You're totally crazy!!"

"H, cool it, it's okay," Yariv answered through clenched teeth, trying to suppress the wave of laughter that came over him. "Do you remember I told you that in Khartoum there was another member of our force who was dealing with similar activities, but from a different angle? Well, this was the guy. His name is Jack, and we have known each other for years. I had no doubt that he understood right away who you were and was happy to take part in a short, intimate practical joke."

Jack was part of Uri's team, which managed to move thousands of Jews through Khartoum quietly, consistently and with hardly any trouble. The Jews left Sudan in small groups in the guise of Christian refugees, under the umbrella of a humanitarian organization that didn't bother about small details. In the Mossad headquarters the performance of the "legitimate" route run by Jack and his men was summed up and compared to the one run by Danny and Yariv. The bottom line was that the former was cheaper and more efficient. Their mode of operation was less heroic than ours, involved fewer James Bond-like tactics, and above all didn't employ the vast and complicated coordination required between the Mossad, the navy and the air force. Small-scale operations naturally involved small-scale risks.

At this point, it's worth noting that during the first days of the Sudan operation, after Danny produced the first evidence of the presence of Beta Yisrael people in the refugee camps, the option of organizing an airlift to secretly remove Jews disguised as Christian refugees was continually explored.

Arie, a short, energetic and resourceful man, was sent to Khartoum to convince the Sudanese government officials with promises and bribes to allow Jews to leave in that manner.

Under an assumed identity, he managed to meet with one of the top officials and carefully unfolded his idea, including hints of hefty "compensation," enough to ensure a comfortable existence for this official in Europe for the rest of his life.

The latter's reaction was firm. "I advise you to leave Sudan within twelve hours," he said, "unless you want to become familiar with our jail system from the inside — and for many years."

But since that incident, much water had flowed through the Nile. Millions of refugees flooded Sudan. The civil war in the south of the country drained the public coffers, and soon undermined the position of the ruler, Jaafar Nimeiri, and his supporters. Because of the famine in Africa and the hardships in Sudan, Nimeiri's future depended almost entirely on further economic and humanitarian aid from the United States.

I won't expand on the topic of US-Israeli relations, nor about the extent of relations between the intelligence communities of the two countries. I will just say that following the Mossad headquarters decision to recheck the option of an airlift from Khartoum, a formal request was handed to Washington for help in the humanitarian mission of extricating refugees from hunger-stricken Africa. The request was promptly granted.

In September 1984 a member of the US embassy staff in the capital, Khartoum, submitted a plan for taking the Jews out of Sudan, according to an investigative report published about a year later in the *Los Angeles Times*:

The plan was the brainchild of Jerry Weaver, 46, a former college lecturer, and then coordinator of refugee affairs at the embassy. Several days later, General Omar el Tayeb, Nimeiri's No 2, met with Hume Horan, the American ambassador in Khartoum.

"We are in desperate need of assistance," said the general.

"We shall be happy to assist, not only with money and food, but also in evacuating part of the refugees from Sudan," the diplomat said.

Tayeb understood full well what was at stake, so he posed a tough condition: his men would oversee the evacuation and the transfer of the refugees must be to Europe — and nowhere else. He also requested funding for his people involved in the operation and "percentages" for himself. Another strict condition laid by Tayeb was complete secrecy. One word to the press or other media would immediately terminate the operation.

The plan was named "Operation Moses."

"Tayeb received at least two million dollars straight into a London bank account," said Kamal Ghazoly, a member of an official inquiry commission set up after the conclusion of Operation Moses. During an interview with Christopher Dickey, the AP correspondent in Khartoum, Ghazoly listed the rest of the funding arrangements: "Full funding of all expenses connected with the operation, such as rental of buses for transfer of the refugees from Gedaref to Khartoum, financing the purchase of special vehicles and communication equipment for the operation, to remain with Tayeb's security forces after the operation, and a small executive aircraft (which had nothing to do with the operation, but was nevertheless 'nice to have')."

In the early planning stages the Israeli charter airline Maof was considered as the airlifting candidate. The company was selected because it was registered in the United States and its aircraft bore American "tail numbers" (registration). All Maof pilots were Israeli Air Force veterans, rendering easier coordination and common language between the Mossad and the pilots. However, a day before the first flight to Sudan, Yariv received an order from the head of the Mossad to stop negotiations with Maof and seek an alternative, apparently due to pressure from El Al. The national carrier did whatever it could to strangle the small, agile competitor. It feared that the five million dollars promised to Maof for the operation would enable the company to make a turnaround. Operation Moses was thus put off for a few precious weeks, even before the operation got under way.

The Mossad approached a small airline named TEA (Trans European Airlines), Brussels based and owned by a warmhearted Jew. The owner gladly committed himself to the cause and put his Boeing 707 aircraft at the disposal of the airlift.

Yariv and his team worked out the fine details. One of the senior men in Mossad operations, whose name is withheld for obvious reasons, was dispatched under cover to Khartoum to work in conjunction with Weaver.

Operation Moses started on November 21, 1984, wrote the *Los Angeles Times*. Weaver and his assistants prepared a meeting spot for the Jews in a compound at the outskirts of Gedaref. Hundreds of Jews swarmed the compound, hoping to get aboard one of the four Sudanese military buses Weaver had coordinated. "The time was six in the evening, pitch dark. The Sudanese were becoming nervous, I was on edge, and the anxious Jews boarding the buses were certainly nervous as well," Weaver described that evening's events.

"By six thirty we crammed God knows how many people into the buses in an effort to leave the place. People were running after us. It was total chaos. The drive to Khartoum took several hours. Security men from Tayeb's organization speeded the convoy through traffic police roadblocks and assembled the refugees on the far and deserted side of Khartoum Airport."

"They were sitting quietly," Weaver recounted. "We could hear no noise. Once or twice a baby was heard crying, but it stopped right away."

The Belgian aircraft landed at 01:20. The pilot and stewardesses were shocked upon seeing their passengers. They had been told that they were going to evacuate refugees, but they didn't expect a crowd of 250 men, women, children and elderly people, dressed in tatters. Many appeared sick. They sat two or three per seat, frightened. On board were an Israeli doctor and a Mossad escort.

But the airliner didn't take off.

"Sorry," the captain said. "We have 250 people on board but the aircraft has only 220 oxygen masks. It's against the law. I can't take off."

Yehuda, the senior Mossad escort, looked the captain up and down and told him in a quiet but forceful voice: "Go right ahead, make a selection [he used this loaded word deliberately]. You decide who lives and who dies."

The captain turned pale, hesitating.

"If you don't return to the cabin and start the engines, I'll throw you off the aircraft and get another pilot to fly it," bellowed the Mossad man, convincingly. The first Operation Moses flight left Khartoum at 02:40. After a brief stopover in Europe, the aircraft landed in Israel the same day. "The airplane stank to high heaven. The immigrants didn't know how to use the lavatories, which got clogged. The Belgian stewardesses weren't up to handling such passengers, but to their credit, it must be said that they worked with great devotion," said a Jewish Agency official who greeted the immigrants at Ben-Gurion International Airport.

The airliner was hosed down, refueled and flew back to Khartoum via Europe. The airlift had begun. Operation Moses was under way.

"During forty-seven days, on twenty-eight covert flights, the aircraft carried more than six thousand Ethiopian Jews," the *Los Angeles Times* reported. The TEA airliners landed in Athens, Herkalion, Rome and Brussels, under the agreement with Tayeb, and only then proceeded to Israel.

Chapter 41

The last time I arrived in Sudan was in December 1984, three years after I first landed there. In the preceding days, I closely read the news stories that piled up in the censor's tray in the *Maariv* newsroom. There were dozens of them. The censor's efforts to prevent leaks about Operation Moses resembled the tale about the Dutch boy who tried to plug a leak in a dam with his finger. Half the nation knew about the operation. Nearly every evening a planeload of Ethiopian immigrants would land at Ben-Gurion Airport. They would be taken to a nearby military air base and from there to absorption centers, to join thousands of their brethren who had arrived by air and sea in previous operations or through "legitimate" and "semi-legitimate" channels.

The Jewish Agency, after years of near total inaction, mobilized all its workers to make the immigrants' integration easier. The Israeli-based foreign press corps was privy to the secret, but held back in deference to the censor's request not to undermine the rescue operation.

As part of the effort to prevent the media from leaking the story, the Mossad invited the senior editors of all the Israeli newspapers to witness the arrival of one of the TEA aircraft at Ben-Gurion Airport. As they watched the frail Ethiopian Jews disembark and kneel to kiss the Israeli ground, a scene that brought tears to the eyes of all present, the Mossad people emphasized the importance of their restraint: "If you mention this operation even slightly, thousands of these people will die of disease and hunger in Sudan," they were told.

This time I left for Sudan fully updated. The nervousness and concern that accompanied the first door-opening moment at Khartoum International Airport were only a memory; I was totally

205

relaxed now. And not just because of accumulated past experience, but mainly because of the clear knowledge that this time I'd be arriving as part of a well-organized R & R.

To clarify: Operation Moses was completely compartmentalized from the Arous Holiday Village activity. The crews organizing the convoys from Gedaref to the TEA airliners in Khartoum were not connected in any way with the team that continued to operate the village, thereby maintaining an extra parallel operational option.

In December 1984 I was sent to Sudan in the capacity of instructor/entertainer to beef up the village workforce, which had to cope with an influx of guests. This may not conform with the heroic tales and the halo of covert activity, but this mission was different. We were not intended to engage in any operational activity, but rather in a lot of sports, food, and parties to music presented by the best disc jockey in Khartoum, who was flown to the village especially for this purpose.

During that time we arranged several very decadent dinners in honor of Christmas and New Year's Eve. There was famine in vast parts of Sudan, but not along the coast and certainly not in the Arous Holiday Village, whose operation did not depend on the cash flow it generated.

The tables keeled under the burden of grouper fish and giant lobsters, rice dishes, mountains of *dakim-dakim* french fries, piles of salads and a selection of choice pastries. Sudan's new laws forbade serving alcoholic beverages, so the guests were forced to settle for local Cola, soda water and a special kind of tea — *chai Fransawi* — that helped keep morale up. This "tea" was introduced in the village following stories by well-informed people in the Gulf sheikhdoms that the hotels there were serving their guests "French tea" — superb French cognac poured from decanters into tea glasses, so as not to antagonize the Islamic religious leaders. We didn't have French cognac, but our crew managed to acquire a large supply of Eritrean brandy which was quickly renamed *"chai Fransawi."*

The vacationers roster featured a number of diplomatic families from Khartoum, two senior Sudanese officials who started imbibing *chai Fransawi* at ten o'clock in the morning, and a Danish milk processing expert and his adolescent daughter whom Gidi, the youngest member of the crew, tried to seduce with tales of courageous fights with sharks.

The local crew, working around the clock, managed to contribute to the holiday spirit. After a group sing-along covering favorites from "I'm Dreaming of a White Christmas" to "Jingle Bells," the workers laid on a medley of Edandawa tribal dances, and to round off the long day, broke into energetic dancing into the night to tunes played on the sophisticated audio system of Sudan's best DJ.

"I've had a good time in many places in my life, but never quite like this," the German deputy military attaché told me, flushed red as a crab and poached by the sun. He had bad cramps from the snap windsurfing course I gave him in the lagoon. The Bundeswehr officer was elated to find a German-speaker in the area, and with each gulp of French tea his love grew for the village, its operators and me — his German-speaking windsurfing instructor. During his last night, after downing a whole pitcher of *chai Fransawi*, he made me swear by all that's dear to me to visit him in Bavaria. I, of course, had no intention of ever popping up on his doorstep and delving into nostalgic tales about the sweet days of Arous. I only hope that after the end of his term in Sudan, he didn't try to locate me at the phony address I gave him in a European country.

A few days after the last guest left the village, I flew to Khartoum on my way to Israel via Europe. As we waited in our villa in Khartoum for the Swissair flight to Zurich, I heard the details that led to the publication of reports about Operation Moses in the Israeli and international media and on the official Israel Radio.

It turned out that *Nekudah*, the magazine of Jewish settlers in the West Bank and the Gaza Strip, published an article, based on interviews with some officials, saying that "Most of Ethiopia's Jews have already reached Israel." The editor of *Nekudah* decided that the censor's reign did not include his insignificant magazine, and never even passed the contents of the interview through the usual military censor channel.

"If such an article is published, then it is a go-ahead for the story to come out," the foreign correspondents concluded, rushing to the phones and teleprinters. They didn't lack for details. Back on November 20, the Jewish Agency in New York had already run a statement from the Jewish Agency's president, Arye Dulzin, seeking to justify its demand from American Jews to raise a hundred million dollars. "I'm not at liberty to discuss this matter publicly," the statement said, "but one of the oldest Jewish tribes is about to return to its homeland."

That was the cue for New York's *Jewish Press* weekly to run the story of the repatriation of Ethiopian Jews from Sudan. On December 12, reports appeared in the *New York Times* and the *Boston Globe*. Only a special request by the Israeli government prevented the newspapers from expanding on the reports. Meanwhile, planeloads of refugees landed in Israel day in, day out. Just at that point, in early January, *Nekudah* ran its article.

Reuters news agency used the slip of tongue, and the headline "Operation Moses" graced the front pages of every newspaper around the world.

Jaafar Nimeiri and General Omar el Tayeb had no choice but to immediately bar TEA aircraft flights from Khartoum.

In the office of operations command the details of a flight that was intended to leave Saturday night, January 5, 1985, were already posted: Brussels-Khartoum-Brussels. Escorts: Senior Jewish Agency officials Arye Dulzin and Yehuda Dominitz.

The aircraft never took off, nor did the following flights, and all because of some senior officials' urge to shoot their mouths off, which sank the entire operation, causing thousands of Jews to remain stranded on Sudanese soil.

Chapter 42

Hundreds of Sudanese soldiers were present at the Khartoum airport that week in early January 1985. Everyone was nervous. Passport and customs control dragged out demonstrably, unlike earlier times when a respectable passport and a white face would take you to the departure hall in no time. For the first time since I had begun operating in Sudan, one officer demanded emphatically to see the contents of my wallet and compared them to the number I entered in the "foreign currency declaration — export" form. The smell of a military coup wafted in the air.

A collective sigh of relief of some two hundred passengers filled the cabin of the Airbus airliner the moment its wheels broke contact with the asphalt runway of Khartoum. The well-groomed stewardess didn't serve *chai Fransawi* to the passengers. This was replaced by beer and real wine. And newspapers. *Nueue Zuricher Zeitung* and the *International Herald Tribune* flashed the Operation Moses story across the top of their front pages.

Several hours later we were in Europe en route to Israel.

I resumed work with *Maariv*. At the end of each shift I made sure, as I had been accustomed to, to go over the contents of the censor's tray. I was worried about my buddies who were left in Khartoum and Arous. The news from there was not good.

Jaafar Nimeiri had become the Arab world's punching bag. He was assailed from every direction over his collaboration with the Zionists and for dispatching new immigrants to Israel, who would serve in the Zionist occupation army in the future.

Nimeiri didn't fail to respond. "We don't run checks on individual refugees," he said in an interview with the Lebanese newspaper. "I have more than one million refugees. We don't ask them if they are Muslim, Christian, pagan or Jewish."

Nimeiri assailed his critics in the Arab countries for their indifference to the fate of the refugees inundating Sudan. "Sudan doesn't place obstacles in the way of whoever seeks to leave it. We regard this as a prime humanitarian action. The entire world is talking about help for the refugees, but how many of them were absorbed in other countries? Almost none. In Saudi Arabia and the rich Gulf States — four thousand. And the West is in no hurry to take them either — twenty-two hundred in the United States, two hundred in Canada, ten in Britain, three in Australia and only one in Norway!"

Nimeiri's explanations did not improve his position in the Arab world. Domestic tension in Sudan increased, and with it the concern for the fate of a few hundred Jews who were stranded in the compound near Gedaref because of the uncontrollable loose tongues of some Israeli officials. Many thousands of Jews were still in Sudan at the time, but the locals couldn't identify them as Jews. However, at the time Operation Moses was stopped, there were a few hundred Jews awaiting the next two TEA flights. These were known as Jews to the few Sudanese taking part in Operation Moses, and were therefore in great danger. Their salvation came directly from the White House in Washington, or more precisely from Vice President George Bush's office.

What's the connection between the vice president of the world's greatest power and several hundred miserable refugees in Africa? From various accounts at the time it emerges that Bush did not remain indifferent to the Mossad's exceptional activity in Africa. Bush, who had served as director of the CIA (the Central Intelligence Agency), was appreciative of the readiness of the Israeli government to put the lives of secret agents and military personnel on the line in order to rescue the refugees from Africa. His appreciation was bolstered in the face of the indifference of the world, which calmed its conscience by organizing huge rock concerts and fund-raisers.

Bush took personal interest in the progress of Operation Moses and was generally familiar with the Mossad activity in parallel channels, such as the Arous Holiday Village.

Several weeks after the Operation Moses flights were grounded, in February 1985, General el Tayeb was invited to Washington. The *Los Angeles Times* researchers wrote that CIA director William Colby explained to el Tayeb that the US administration was ready to help solve the Jewish refugee problem quietly, thereby easing the pressure on Nimeiri. El Tayeb took the hint and updated his president accordingly.

In early March, when George Bush came to Sudan on a working visit, he promised Nimeiri extensive economic aid in return for his approval of an American-sponsored operation to rescue the Jews who were stranded in Gedaref because of the suspension of Operation Moses.

Indeed, a few days later, seven Hercules transports from an American transport squadron based at Ramstein Air Base in Germany landed in Gedaref's small military airfield. Under the protection of General el Tayeb's security services and a small team of Mossad operatives, they arranged the removal of Jews from Tawawa camp to the airfield, where Ethiopian immigration activists made sure that their planes were boarded only by Jews and members of their families. Unlike the TEA airplanes which flew to Israel via Europe, the Americans took off from Sudan directly to the Israeli Ramon Air Base in the Negev desert.

Many Jews who were hoping to be rescued by Operation Moses remained stranded in Sudan. Some were ill, some preferred to await the arrival in Sudan of the remainder of their families from Ethiopia, and some were non-Jewish kin, the Falashmura, whose eligibility to immigrate to Israel under the Law of Return sparked a major controversy among Ethiopian émigrés in the 1990s.

Chapter 43

Within days after the American airlift, the Nimeiri era in Sudan ended. "Today, April 6, 1985, we unseated Nimeiri the dictator. We, a group of army officers, will restore democracy and have our homeland ruled by the will of the people," Omdurman Radio announced. Sixteen years of rule by the General, who was one of the most committed US allies in this part of the world, came to an end.

The deposed ruler heard this statement in Washington in the midst of an official visit, during which he won countless kudos for his part in the rescue of the Ethiopian refugees. This activity contributed in large measure to his downfall, but he probably found solace in the fact that this activity prompted President Ronald Reagan to invite him to Washington, thereby sparing him contact with the noose the conspirators had readied for him.

Unlike Nimeiri, who took a pro-Western policy, the coup leaders opted to embrace radical Islam and other extremist elements in the Arab world, such as Muammar Khadaffi, the Libyan ruler, as their role models. Supporters of the old regime, General el Tayeb included, were arrested, tortured and spilled everything they knew about the exploits of Nimeiri and his cronies, including Operation Moses and the American rescue airlift.

"Several days after Nimeiri's removal, Libyan intelligence experts arrived in Khartoum," wrote the *Los Angeles Times* years later, appearing to have specialized in exposing secrets connected with Mossad activity in Sudan. "It was clear to the leaders of the military junta that a unit of Israeli intelligence was active in Khartoum," the newspaper reported. "The task of uncovering its members, thereby giving a major propaganda boost to the new regime, was given to Khaddafi's intelligence experts."

Three Mossad operatives were then in Khartoum. Mano was one of them. Debriefings conducted some time later indicated that he was responsible, at least partially, due to lack of vigilance, for the uncovering of the Mossad front office in Khartoum.

Fortunately for Mano and his men, the Americans had an active espionage branch in Khartoum. Years later, the *Los Angeles Times* revealed how the Israelis were rescued, as follows:

> The Mossad agents ran for their lives. They ran through Khartoum's busy streets, under the noses of Sudanese secret service and its Libyan allies. Their cover — European businessmen — was blown and their operational center disguised as a private business office was uncovered too. The Israelis were able to save only the secret communication equipment and then fled for their lives under cover of night. Their destination: the home of Milton Bearden, chief of the CIA station in Khartoum.
>
> "I felt they were my comrades-at-arms," recalled Bearden, who quit the Agency in 1994. He took care of the three Israelis.

Meanwhile the Mossad dispatched Moise to Khartoum to try to rescue the three, but Sudanese intelligence blew his cover and he too joined Bearden's three fugitives.

"For the next thirty days, Bearden hid the four Israelis. He transferred them in a US embassy minibus from one safe house to another, thereby sparing them arrest and possibly death," according to the *Los Angeles Times*. Monitoring Sudanese security service networks, the CIA crew knew exactly where the Sudanese and Libyans were focusing their search. "We were ahead of them but the net became tighter and tighter," Bearden said. "We had to get them out of Khartoum."

According to the American newspaper, the CIA technicians built four special boxes. Israelis will recall a box from a different story. In the 1960s an Italian policeman heard suspicious sounds coming from a heavy crate brought by an Egyptian embassy driver to Rome's international airport. Over the Egyptian protestations that it contained diplomatic mail, the policemen opened the box. Inside they found an Israeli national, Mordechai Luk, whom Egyptian intelligence sought to kidnap to Cairo.

The Israelis who found shelter with Bearden were "packed" in those four special boxes, equipped with oxygen bottles. The boxes were packed and labeled as diplomatic mail, put on a vehicle and, escorted by three members of the CIA station, were loaded onto an American C-141 transport aircraft that had been sent to Khartoum expressly for that purpose.

Sudanese intelligence appeared to have sniffed out what was happening and even tried to delay the United States Air Force C-141 departure.

"Don't ask for an OK and don't talk to the tower," Bearden ordered the pilots. "Start the engines and take off for Nairobi." The pilots did just that, chased by a trail of screams, curses and threats from the control tower.

Once the aircraft landed in Nairobi, the four passengers, all huddled and concealed inside the boxes wearing nothing but underpants — except Uri who insisted on shorts, saying, "I'd rather be dressed in case the Sudanese get us" — disembarked. They were given fresh passports and proceeded home, to Israel.

The four were saved. Warm cables of thanks were sent from Tel Aviv to Washington extolling the close cooperation between the two espionage outfits, and also containing beautiful prose about a common future and the camaraderie of those bearing arms.

Five months later, a US Navy analyst named Jonathan Pollard was arrested in Washington on suspicion of spying for Israel. Oded Granot, then *Maariv* correspondent in Washington, reported that the heads of the American intelligence community were furious with their ungrateful Israeli counterparts, who ran an agent in the heart of an American intelligence organization.

No one had any idea what "ungratefulness" the Americans were talking about, except for four Mossad operatives who spent a few hours of their lives in small boxes, and a few dozen confidants.

Chapter 44

One April day in 1985, toward the end of a routine evening shift on the *Maariv* news desk, the phone on my desk rang.

"Gadi, the gang were evacuated tonight from the village. They have just arrived," said Mickey. "We are sitting in Yariv's apartment."

Within minutes I finished editing the stories I was supposed to prepare for the foreign pages, mumbled some excuse and hurried out of there. I raced through the deserted streets.

Despite the late hour, well after midnight, there was a party atmosphere in Yariv's living room. There were many toasts. Jokes were flying in the air; banter and boisterous laughter all attested to great tension dissipating. Here and there the doorbell rang again, and another Sudan veteran came in, hugged those present and heard the details of the miraculous rescue. Following Nimeiri's overthrow, it became clear that it was only a matter of time before Sudanese security services got wise to the true nature of the Arous Holiday Village. The heads of Mossad had no doubt that this mode of operation had ended its useful life and that it was time to clear the village.

"We know that the Israelis who operated the village were evacuated aboard a C-130 transport that landed in the desert," said Kamal Ghazoly, a member of the Sudanese inquiry commission. "The Israelis simply disappeared."

The local workers at the Arous Holiday Village told Sudanese police investigators that at the time only a small team of Europeans were in the village. "The village is empty of guests, and therefore we're using the time to check out new diving sites," the Europeans told them, as they loaded up two Toyota vehicles, a pickup truck and a closed utility vehicle, with diving gear, fuel, a folded boat, food and water.

The version Yariv and his men related absolutely matched the account given by the workers in faraway Sudan.

"Just as we were leaving we managed to see two new tourists arriving at the village. I hope the local workers took good care of them," Yariv said.

The two vehicles drove away from the village. A few hours later, after darkness had set down over the Sudanese desert, some 130 kilometers (eighty miles) north of the holiday village, the voice of the pilot, a veteran of many operations in Sudan, was heard on the radio. A series of pre-agreed signs assured the pilot that the landing site was ready, and that those waiting for him down below were Mossad agents and not a company of Sudanese soldiers.

The C-130 landed and the two vehicles drove up the loading ramp into the aircraft belly.

That same night, a small, quaint convoy moved on the roads in central Israel. Escorted by a police squad car, Yariv and his men drove the two vehicles, still bearing Sudanese registration numbers, up to the Mossad headquarters. The vehicles were concealed in the agency garage and the crew members proceeded to the impromptu meet in Yariv's apartment.

"That's it. The village chapter is over," Yariv said, raising a toast "to the operations that were, those that will come, and I hope our loyal employees, Abu Medina, Muhammed, Ahmed, Hassan, Ali and the others will weather this change in the history of Arous peacefully."

Chapter 45

The closing of the Arous Holiday Village and the rescue of the four Israelis from Khartoum did not put an end to the Mossad activities in that part of the world. Jews continued to stream from war-torn Ethiopia into Sudan, which was relatively safe. To pull them out, new teams were set up whose members managed to operate across Sudan thanks to an appropriate cover story. Jerry and Daniko, for instance, visited refugee camps clandestinely and in a series of operations managed to extricate hundreds of Jews in small groups.

At this point a new mode of operation was adopted by Yariv, with part of the rescuers' crew slipping into Sudan by sea, and leaving on Israeli Air Force C-130 Hercules aircraft with the new immigrants, without Sudanese authorities knowing that they had ever stepped on Sudanese soil. Then a new team, headed by Eyal, continued to pull Jews out of Sudan through March 1990.

Four years after the option of repatriating Jews through the holiday village or in mass operations like Operation Moses fell through, and in light of the astounding changes that characterized the world in the late 1980s, an opportunity emerged to fly out the remainder of Ethiopian Jews, an estimated fifteen thousand souls, directly from Addis Ababa.

That window of opportunity opened in November 1989. While the world's eyes were focused on the historic collapse of the Communist regimes in Europe, an official announcement from the Ethiopian government reached Jerusalem unexpectedly. "The government of Ethiopia has decided to resume diplomatic relations with Israel," the announcement said. The background to this about-face, following a complete break of relations between the two countries in the 1970s, stemmed from the growing isolation of

Mengistu and his junta, which was a result of far-reaching changes beginning at the end of the 1980s. Political and economic hardship forced the Communist countries to cut back on the assistance they provided. The battles in Eritrea and Tigre got fiercer, and famine again threatened to kill millions of farmers in the country's remotest areas.

Only those who have worked in the Third World know how deep-rooted is the belief in the unshakeable might of the Jewish-Israeli lobby in Washington. Mengistu thus decided, on the advice of his counselor Kesse Kabeda, a Hebrew-speaker who once studied in Jerusalem, that the road to breaking the boycott the West had imposed on him ran through Israel.

Several hours after the Ethiopian foreign ministry announcement came out, my editors at *Maariv* assigned me to be the first Israeli news correspondent to go to Addis Ababa. I agreed, but made it clear to them that my departure could not be immediate since we had to fly to Europe, get an Ethiopian visa in an Ethiopian embassy, receive the appropriate vaccinations and make other necessary arrangements.

"There's no time," the editor cut me short. "I know the competition. They have certainly sent someone on his way already. You have experience from previous work. I don't care how, but I want you to be the first to reach Addis Ababa. Don't let us down."

I accepted the challenge, not least because it would make it possible for me to close a personal cycle: after such intensive activity extricating Ethiopian Jews from Sudan, I was glad of the opportunity to visit their homeland, which until then had been almost entirely closed to Israelis.

I turned to my loyal friend Yagil for help. The resourceful young man moonlighted as a night editor in addition to his work as a knowledgeable travel agent familiar with all the ins and outs of the trade. A few telephone calls and clarifications revealed that an Ethiopian Airlines flight was scheduled to land in Cairo on its way from Moscow to Addis Ababa the same night.

I put together my plan.

From experience I knew that a well-phrased letter on expensive-looking stationery could open doors, so I availed myself of several versions.

I reached the Rafah border crossing minutes before closing time. I had no permit from the army to let me leave the country, and only an urgent telephone call persuaded the policeman to let me leave Israel's borders. On the Egyptian side of the terminal, I hired a taxi that looked new and reliable, and we started on our way. The driver, of Palestinian descent, raced along the Sinai road almost like Ayrton Senna, the Formula One champion, spurred by the promise of a fat bonus if we made it to Cairo International Airport on time. As he was driving, he cursed the Egyptian policemen who bullied him at every roadblock only because he was a Palestinian. I heard him curse and bitch, but did not respond. I was trying to take in a few hours of sleep.

The Ethiopian Airlines station manager at Cairo Airport was not impressed by the flight ticket I showed him. "I'm sorry," he said, "I have a standing order not to board passengers who have no entry visa to Ethiopia."

"But I was invited by your government," I insisted, presenting him with one of the documents which were printed in Tel Aviv in the name of the Ethiopian ambassador to the United Nations. The document, about which the ambassador knew nothing, of course, was addressed to "Whom it may concern," requesting to render assistance to an Israeli journalist covering the revival of relations between the two countries with a common past...et cetera, et cetera.

I boarded the plane, which was packed with Russian army officers returning to Ethiopia from home furlough. The Soviet Union still kept thousands of "advisors" in Ethiopia in an effort to decide the civil war in favor of Mengistu. Stasi officials, the East German security police, were in charge of domestic security in Ethiopia. I met some of them indirectly at a later stage.

Most of the Russian passengers were already full of quantities of vodka they had downed during the first leg of the flight. But they were very kind to me, and thanks to two of them I managed to clear the first hurdle at the Addis Ababa airport: the Ethiopian Health Ministry counter.

I did not have a vaccination booklet, and was therefore banned from setting foot on Ethiopian soil. But as the Ethiopian immigration officer was studying the documents of two corpulent Russian officers, I used the opportunity and sneaked to the border control counter.

The declarations of friendship and the warm hug I gave the duty officer did not change his lukewarm attitude toward me because of the lack of an entry visa in my passport. After two hours of negotiation, an examination of the letters I presented, and consulting by telephone with an anonymous superior, the officer decided to allow me to enter the country. But he made sure that I realized that he was only granting me a temporary permit. My passport was impounded, and in its place I received a crumpled piece of paper, saying that I may stay in the country for one week only, and only within the limits of the capital.

Addis Ababa used to be a beautiful city, graced by wide avenues built by the Italians, public parks, sumptuous buildings housing officials from the Organization of African Unity, and beautiful villas — all alongside unbelievable poverty. The streets were packed with lame, blind and disabled people of all kinds, as well as prostitutes, mostly young girls.

A huge statue of Lenin overlooked a vast square where Mengistu used to hold his incessant military parades. A huge poster bearing the somber face of Mengistu, who had dreamed about transplanting Marxism to Africa, hung above the main podium. "Even Lenin wants out," said the cab driver who took me to the Hilton Hotel. "Look closer at the statue, and you'll notice he is lifting his foot in the direction of the airport."

Great. I had arrived in Addis Ababa. What next? I didn't know a soul. There was still no official Israeli representative. "What to do?" I said to myself with despair, as I was drinking a cold beer in the bar.

I sank into doleful thoughts, and as I gazed down I noticed a pair of sports shoes approaching me — not just sports trainers, but Israeli-made "Gali" shoes. I caught the hand of the man who was wearing the shoes. "I don't know you, but I desperately need help," I said in Hebrew.

The man, about sixty, lean and bronzed, turned to me with a frightened look in his eyes.

"How do you know I'm Israeli? And who are you, anyway?"

Pointing at his shoes, I told him who I was and what I was doing in the Hilton bar.

I have always spoken volumes about the value of coincidence, and the Gali shoes story bore me out yet again. It turned out that the Israeli, a resident of the Tel Aviv suburb of Petah Tikva, was also a French passport holder. For nearly four decades he had been raising crocodiles on a number of farms across Ethiopia and selling their skins in France. "I know everybody, from Emperor Haile Selassie to Mengistu," he said in what later proved to be no idle boasting at all.

The Israeli crocodile grower opened doors for me in Addis Ababa. My requests for an interview with Mengistu or one of his ministers were turned down outright, for fear of adverse reaction in the Arab world. But I did have plenty of meetings with senior officials for background. I also managed to make contact with Ethiopian Jews, of which several hundred had gathered in the capital waiting for better days.

"Our neighbors are pestering us," they said. "We miss our family members who immigrated to Israel via Sudan and want to reunite with them in Zion."

They unfolded difficult stories about persecution and poverty but were full of praise for the activities of the Joint, a Jewish aid agency, which distributed food, medicines and clothes. "Tell our government [their words: our government] to bring us over quickly, home, to Jerusalem," they pleaded quietly, fearing the big ears of the local security services, who were trained by the East German Stasi secret police.

An Ethiopian domestic security service unit was sitting on my tail throughout my stay in Addis Ababa. Being a graduate of Mossad operations I had no trouble spotting them. Perhaps due to budget constraints, their carpool consisted only of two beat-up Japanese vehicles, thus making my job of exposing them real child's play.

By contrast, I couldn't but admire the stamina of the surveillance crew, particularly the "parallels," those who worked the streets parallel to my walking route and had to cover long distances running — not a mean feat in the thin air of Addis Ababa, located two thousand meters (6500 feet) above sea level. Who knows, perhaps the Ethiopian security service surveillance detail actually served as a training ground for the gifted athletes who later won many medals in Olympic long-distance running events?

To the credit of the Ethiopians, they discovered soon enough that someone else was taking part in the surveillance fest. Returning from another day of walking about town, I noticed the Hilton Hotel security officer huddled with someone I readily identified as the head of the Ethiopian surveillance detail. "Mr. Shimron," he told me in a quiet voice, wearing a somber expression. "We received information that Palestine Liberation Organization men are taking undue interest in you. For your own safety, we advise you to leave the country as soon as possible. For your information, there is a flight from Addis Ababa to Cairo, and you have already been booked on that flight."

I took stock of the situation quickly. Despite the polite words, it was not difficult to understand that the authorities had decided to deport me. Truth be told, I didn't regret it, because I had already sent out the journalistic material I had. In the meantime the reports from Ethiopia had been downgraded into the inside pages, and rightly so, because it was then that the Berlin Wall came down. Ethiopia's official media did not bother to apprise the residents of this historic event, which had devastating repercussions for the future of Mengistu's regime. Only those who listened to the BBC or other foreign stations heard about the hordes of Germans crossing through the Brandenburg Gate and hopping over the wall that had divided Berlin since 1961.

The following day I was aboard the flight. My passport in my pocket bore an official Ethiopian stamp: "The bearer may not make a return visit to Ethiopia."

"Never mind," I thought to myself. "If I do want to visit here again, I'll simply change passports."

I tried to doze off, and therefore could hardly hear the captain's voice on the public address system.

"Ladies and gentlemen, we must land because of a technical problem."

"Where are we landing? What happened?" I worriedly asked the passenger sitting next to me, a stunning Ethiopian woman, dressed with chic.

"He said it is a minor problem, that we are flying now over Sudan, and are going to land in Khartoum," she replied with the impatience of a passenger about to miss a connecting flight in Cairo.

My beating heart could be heard all over the cabin.

Khartoum? Of all places? What the hell should I do now? Ask for the captain's protection? Or perhaps it's better not to stick out? And what should I do if the problem was serious and we would have to spend the night in the Khartoum Hilton? I had an Israeli passport and there was every chance that wanted posters with my face emblazoned on them graced the walls of the police station at the airport, albeit with an assumed name. My face had not changed since my last visit four years previously. What would I do if Hassan, the representative of our phony company, who might have continued to make a living as an airport fixer, identified me all of a sudden?

I decided to keep my counsel for the time being, maintain a low profile and wait for developments. I asked the stewardess to quickly bring me a glass of whiskey.

Before landing, the airplane flew in a wide arc over Khartoum. From my window the Sudanese capital looked exactly like it did the first time I landed here in December 1981 on a KLM flight from Amsterdam. I saw the Blue Nile and the White Nile and the city center, still bearing the hallmarks of colonial planning, as well as countless grey and brown houses planted in the yellow plain, interspersed with occasional green patches.

The plane taxied along the runway, coming to a halt at the terminal building, with which I was very familiar.

"Ladies and gentlemen," the captain announced again, "at this stage you are requested to remain on board until we find out the exact nature of the problem."

I sank deep into my seat, trying to blend with the seat color, awaiting the decision of the Sudanese mechanics. The pretty stewardesses made the rounds along the aisles offering cold and hot drinks. Local sanitation workers came on board to collect the cans of drinks and paper bags from the passengers.

A good sign? A bad sign? For a moment I conjured up the image of the senior Sudanese cabinet minister of the old regime, who plied us with forbidden whiskey from the caches in his back yard, boarding the aircraft as a common sanitation worker, and discovering me, his friend from better days.

I sank even deeper in my seat, and in order to keep my spirits up despite the severity of the situation, took small swigs from my whiskey glass.

"Ladies and gentlemen," the captain's deep voice was heard after an hour-long nerve-racking wait. "I am happy to inform you that the problem has been resolved. We are proceeding on our flight to Cairo, and I apologize on behalf of the company for the delay."

"No need to apologize," I said to myself. "*Yallah* — go on, step on it, close the doors and take off, now."

Several minutes later the aircraft took off and from my small window in the front of the cabin I took a last look at Khartoum disappearing under the cover of dust and haze.

Chapter 46

Resumption of diplomatic relations between Jerusalem and Addis Ababa held a promise of redemption for the Ethiopian Jews. The Israeli embassy in Ethiopia started working vigorously to improve the situation of the Jews in the capital, raising the level of education and offering economic help. The Ethiopian authorities turned a blind eye on this activity in return for a discreet military assistance from Israel to Mengistu's army, mostly in technical areas. But anyone who dreamed of a massive exodus of Jews following the resumption of relations was proven wrong.

"I am the father of the Ethiopian nation," Mengistu said, echoing the same words uttered almost thirty years earlier by Emperor Haile Selassie. "How can I allow one of the Ethiopian peoples to leave the country, particularly in the midst of the bitter struggle we are conducting to preserve the unity of the homeland?"

The time of redemption of the Ethiopian Jews was put off by another two years, up to the last hours of the Mengistu era.

And indeed, one weekend in May 1991, Mengistu's regime, which had drowned this lovely country in rivers of blood and tears, was on the brink of extinction. The Eritrean and Tigrean rebel forces laid siege to Addis Ababa, and it was clear to all that it would fall to them within days, or even hours. With the mediation of Kesse Kabado, the Marxist ruler's Hebrew-speaking advisor, and also thanks to forty million dollars deposited in numbered US and Swiss bank accounts, which assured his economic future, Mengistu permitted Israel to pull the thousands of Jews gathered in the Israeli embassy compound and other safe houses out of the besieged capital. Operation Solomon got under way. Never have so many Israeli airplanes flown in African skies as on Friday, May 24, 1991.

More than fourteen thousand Jews were rescued in less than twenty-four hours in a well-organized airlift. Initially they were evacuated in El Al Boeing 747 jumbo jets, but it soon became apparent that because of their weight, the huge aircraft were damaging the runway. One of these flights set a world record: in the jumbo jet flown by captain Arie Oz, there were 1067 passengers, mostly Jewish refugees, as well as dozens of soldiers and security personnel.

In place of the jumbo, Israel dispatched anything else that could fly to Ethiopia. There were El Al airliners alongside Israeli Air Force C-130 Hercules transports, which made thirty-three runs in total.

Nearly ten years after Danny's first operation, which rescued 164 Ethiopian Jews by way of the Sudanese coast and took them to an Israeli navy ship that waited way out in the Red Sea, the Ethiopian exile ended. The bulk of the community had arrived in Israel. The ancient prophecy passed down through the generations — that one day Ethiopian Jews would return to Jerusalem — had come true.

Chapter 47

The absorption of Ethiopian Jews in Israel was a limited success story. At the end of 1996 the Ethiopian Jewish community numbered some hundred thousand souls, thirty thousand of them Israeli-born "sabras." Sixty percent were under the age of eighteen.

The reports in January 1985 about the emigration of Ethiopian Jews aroused a great deal of excitement in Israel. But after the initial burst of enthusiasm subsided, Israeli society began baring its ugly, racist face.

It started with innocuous jokes: "Why are Ethiopians called Ethiopians? Because they say '*eizeh yoffi, eizeh yoffi* ("how swell, how swell," a pun in Hebrew)' all the time."

Soon less "cute" jokes followed, along the lines of "Why were the Ethiopians brought here? To be spare parts for Yemeni Jews." Then came other racist utterances that would do Ku Klux Klan veterans proud.

Mayors sought to reduce the number of Ethiopian Jews they were to accept in immigrant hostels "in order not to harm the fabric of the population."

The racist battle against Ethiopian Jews was led, woefully, by some prominent rabbis. Years will go by until members of this wonderful community get over the insults suffered at the hands of the rabbinical establishment.

After the State of Israel mobilized the best of its technological and personnel resources to bring the Ethiopian Jews over peacefully to Israel, they faced demands brought up by the rabbis in the name of the "purity of the Jewish people."

The Ethiopians were made to undergo a series of humiliating conversion rituals, including the symbolic letting of blood that substitutes for circumcision in an already-circumcised conversion candidate and immersion in a *mikvah* (ritual bath), in order to placate the rabbis and prevail on them to regard Ethiopian Jews as Jews. The rabbinate also refused to recognize the authority of the *kessim*, the Ethiopian spiritual leaders. Most rabbis in Israel today are loath to officiate at weddings unless the prospective couple has undergone the prescribed litany of humiliations. Only a very small number of truly pious rabbis, headed by Rabbi Chelouche of Netanya, who paradoxically used the very same laws, regulations and stipulations as those paraded by the others, have treated the Ethiopians as human beings and Jews.

In addition to the scandalous attitude of the religious establishment against the Ethiopian Jews, the state, in all its departments, which boasts of its ability to absorb Jews from all over the world, hasn't vindicated itself as far as Ethiopian Jews are concerned.

The absorption of the Beta Yisrael immigration, so disparate from any other wave of immigrants that had ever reached Israel, required special, unconventional arrangements. But these were not made. In traditional Ethiopian society, elderly people enjoyed a special status of respect, which was smashed to bits in the face of the realities of Israeli life, and reduced to dust because of the relatively fast integration of the younger members of the community. Additionally, many members of the community still don't have appropriate housing. They have been stuck for long years in mobile home parks created hastily when they arrived. There have been cases of Israelis verbally abusing and cursing Ethiopian families that moved into neighboring houses.

"We don't want them as neighbors," it was argued in several different versions. "They spend all their time outdoors. Their children are noisy and destroy the lawns, their homes stink of their bread — what do you call it? Injera? They quarrel and shout all the time..."

Employment was another problematic area for the Ethiopians. Many of them, lacking vocational training, work at menial jobs and barely take home the minimum wage set by law.

Most of their number came from remote areas and their encounter with the modern, permissive Israeli society gave them a bad shock. "We had believed that all Jews around the world are black and follow the customs and laws of Jewish orthodoxy," immigrants have related.

Out of considerations linked to the power play within the governing coalition, the community's children were forced into the parochial education system. They were put together in dedicated classes, with inferior teachers and syllabi. True, there were some success stories as well, mainly thanks to the work and dedication of some outstanding teachers and educators, but unfortunately those were exceptions rather than the rule.

"I can't say that I was a happy boy," said Addis Aklum, the first Ethiopian conscript to graduate an officers' training course with an elite army unit — the paratroops. "It started with them sending the sons of the community into religious education, without asking, because no one trusted our being Jews," Aklum told Efrat Michaeli, an Israeli journalist. "I know people who buried their children along the way here only because of this thing called Judaism. And then you arrive here, and some miserable human being calling himself a religious Jew tries to place you under a magnifying glass. If this were to happen today, I would shove his head into a toilet bowl. Really. No mercy. You have to account for everything and every minute you live," he added in the interview. "I wasn't left with a sweet taste in my mouth. One cannot hide it. You either fell apart or survived with scars."

The greatest insult was exposed early in 1996, when the *Maariv* daily newspaper revealed that blood donations taken from Ethiopian immigrants were thrown in the garbage because of the prevalence of AIDS among the immigrants. "It was a misjudgment stemming from a wish to uphold the dignity of the Ethiopians, not to offend them," the director of the blood bank explained, defending the practice.

"We can't openly demonstrate feelings," the Ethiopians say half apologetically. A series of suicides among Ethiopian soldiers bared a pattern of hazing and abuse that preceded that desperate act for some of them. "We take all the insults quietly," said the brother of an Ethiopian soldier who took his own life.

Addis Aklum, the outstanding officer turned businessman, chose a different track. "It will be easier for me to raise my daughter, who was born here, as a black Jew in Addis Ababa than in Israel," he asserted angrily in the interview, attempting to explain why he of all people decided to take his family back to Ethiopia, "to do business and perhaps to return sometime in the future."

Adissu Massala chose another course of action. The feeling of discrimination and the desire to better the state of the community impelled him to run as an independent candidate in the Labor Party primaries, proceeding from there to a seat in the fourteenth Knesset, Israel's parliament. "I represent not only the Ethiopians, but also all the underprivileged in the country," he said upon being sworn in.

But the absorption of Ethiopian Jews is not characterized only by discrimination and deprivation. There are many success stories, growing in number over the years. Surveys conducted among them show satisfaction with their circumstances in general. Despite the difficulties that characterized their integration here, only few consider following Aklum's example and leaving Israel. "There, in Ethiopia, lies our past," said young boys and girls who visited Ethiopia, "but here, in Israel, lies our future."

Today, thousands of Ethiopian Jews study in various universities in Israel. Hundreds of Ethiopian officers — men and women — serve in all branches of the military, and who knows, perhaps one of them is that little boy, with the huge curious eyes, who laughed heartily when I let him play with the steering wheel of the truck in that remote wadi, somewhere in Sudan, and later, when I visited an absorption center, pulled at my shirt tail, saying, "Uncle, I remember you from the red truck in the wadi."

I will remember him to my last day.